ICON KEY

 REVIEW

 EXAMPLES

 DEFINITIONS

 KEY CONCEPTS

 NOTATIONS & FORMULAS

 CRITICAL THINKING

Section 01

1.1 Statistical and Critical Thinking

1.2 Types of Data

1.3 Collecting Sample Data

Companion to *Elementary Statistics*, Thirteenth Edition and the Triola Stats Series, by Mario F. Triola.

What is Statistics?

STATISTICS — The science of planning studies and experiments, obtaining data, and then organizing, summarizing, presenting, analyzing, interpreting, and drawing conclusions based on the data.

DATA — Collections of observations, such as measurements, genders, or survey responses.

Large Collections of Data

POPULATION — The complete collection of all measurements or data that are being considered

PARAMETER — A numerical measurement describing some characteristic of a population.

Collecting Data from a Population

CENSUS

Collection of data from every member of a population.

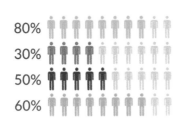

80%
30%
50%
60%

United States Constitution: Article 1, Section 2.3 – Representatives and direct Taxes shall be apportioned … according to their respective Numbers, which shall be determined by adding to the whole Number of free Persons, including those bound to Service for a Term of Years, and excluding Indians not taxes, three fifths of all other Persons. The actual Enumeration shall be made within three Years after the first Meeting of the Congress of the United States, and within every subsequent Term of ten Years, in such Manner as they shall by Law direct. The Number of Representatives shall not exceed one for every thirty Thousand, but each State shall have at Least one Representative…

Three-Fifths Issue

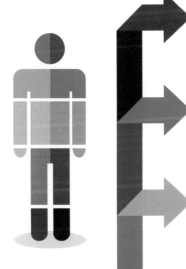

Slaves were treated as property and were not represented by human laws.

Counting slaves would lead to greater slave owner representation, perpetuating the practice of slavery.

Deadlock: North didn't want to count slaves. South would refuse to join if slaves were not counted.

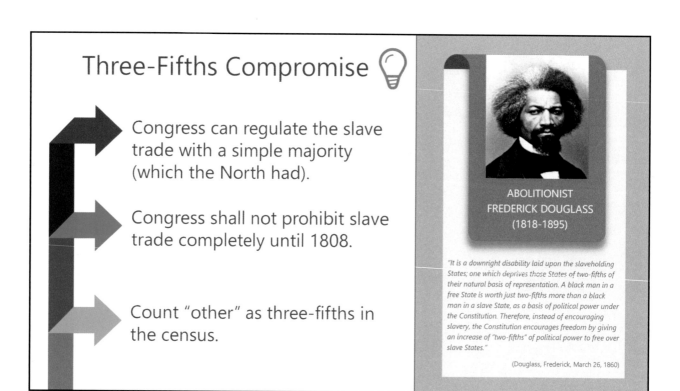

Three-Fifths Compromise

Congress can regulate the slave trade with a simple majority (which the North had).

Congress shall not prohibit slave trade completely until 1808.

Count "other" as three-fifths in the census.

ABOLITIONIST
FREDERICK DOUGLASS
(1818-1895)

"It is a downright disability laid upon the slaveholding States; one which deprives those States of two-fifths of their natural basis of representation. A black man in a free State is worth just two-fifths more than a black man in a slave State, as a basis of political power under the Constitution. Therefore, instead of encouraging slavery, the Constitution encourages freedom by giving an increase of "two-fifths" of political power to free over slave States."

(Douglass, Frederick, March 26, 1860)

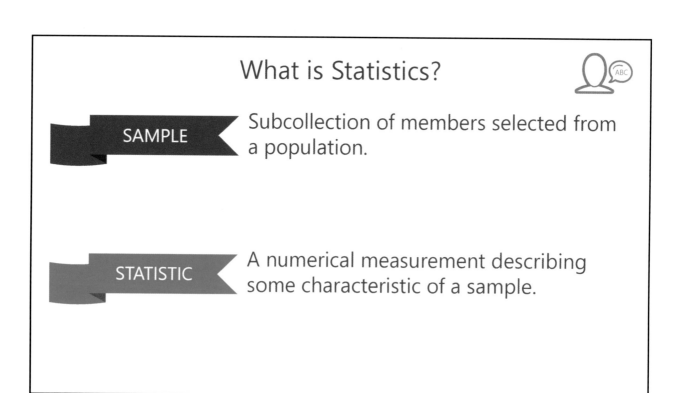

What is Statistics?

SAMPLE Subcollection of members selected from a population.

STATISTIC A numerical measurement describing some characteristic of a sample.

Key Concept

population $\longleftrightarrow$ parameter

sample $\longleftrightarrow$ statistic

The subject of statistics is largely about using sample data to make inferences about an entire population.

Data Types

CATEGORICAL ← EXAMPLE

The gender (male/female) of professional athletes

Categorical (or qualitative or attribute) data consists of names or labels (representing categories).

Shirt numbers on professional athletes uniforms - substitutes for names

QUANTITATIVE ← EXAMPLE

The weights of supermodels

Quantitative (or numerical) data consists of numbers representing counts or measurements.

The ages of respondents

Quantitative Data Further Distinguished....

 DISCRETE EXAMPLE

The number of eggs that a hen lays

Discrete data result when the number of possible values is either a finite number or a 'countable' number (i.e. the number of possible values is 0, 1, 2, 3, . . .).

The number of grains of sand on the beach

 CONTINUOUS EXAMPLE

The amount of milk that a cow produces; e.g. 2.343115 gallons per day

Continuous (numerical) data result from infinitely many possible values that correspond to some continuous scale that covers a range of values without gaps, interruptions, or jumps (measurable).

The speed that your car travels on the freeway; e.g. 74 miles per hour

---

Levels of Measurement (1&2 of 4)

 NOMINAL EXAMPLE

Colors or Men/Women

Nominal level of measurement is characterized by data that consist of names, labels, or categories only, and the data cannot be arranged in an ordering scheme (such as low to high).

Survey responses like yes, no, undecided

 ORDINAL EXAMPLE

Course grades A, B, C, D, or F

Ordinal level of measurement involves data that can be arranged in some order, but differences between data values either cannot be determined or are meaningless.

Likert Scale (a psychometric scale used in questionnaires; e.g. strongly agree, slightly agree, neither agree nor disagree, slightly disagree, strongly disagree)

Levels of Measurement (3&4 of 4)

INTERVAL ← EXAMPLE

Years 1776 and 1492

Interval level of measurement involves data that can be arranged in order and the difference between any two data values is meaningful. However, there is no natural zero starting point (where none of the quantity is present).

 Temperature in Celsius or Fahrenheit

RATIO ← EXAMPLE

Speed, Height, Weight, Volume

Ratio level of measurement the interval level with the additional property that there is also a natural zero starting point (where zero indicates that none of the quantity is present); for values at this level, differences and ratios are meaningful.

Temperature in Kelvin

Accuracy Versus Precision

What is the difference between accuracy and precision?
(Hint: Try using them in sentences...)

ACCURACY

Accuracy describes the nearness of a measurement to the standard or true value, i.e., a highly accurate measuring device will provide measurements very close to the standard, true or known values.

PRECISION

Precision is the degree to which several measurements provide answers very close to each other. It is an indicator of the scatter in the data. The lesser the scatter, higher the precision.

Accuracy Versus Precision

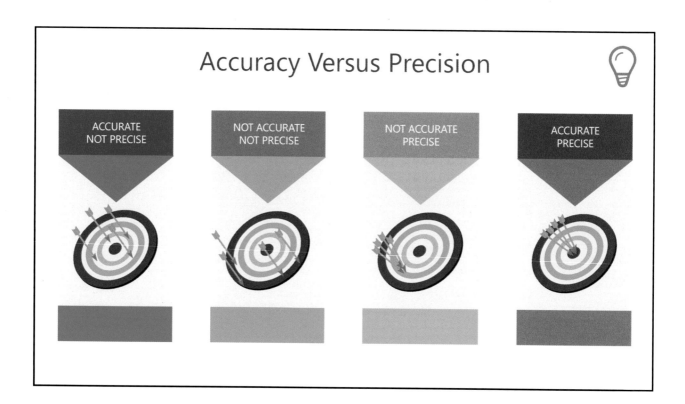

Headlines & Statistics

"28.5714% of LAVC Students love statistics!"
Discuss this statement.

Bad Data Yields Bad Statistics

If sample data are not collected in an appropriate way, the data may be so completely useless that no amount of statistical torturing can salvage them.

The method used to collect sample data influences the quality of the statistical analysis.

Basics of Collecting Data

Statistical methods are driven by the data that we collect. Data is typically obtained from two distinct sources:

OBSERVATIONAL STUDY
Observe and measure specific characteristics without attempting to modify the subjects being studied.

EXPERIMENTAL STUDY
Apply some treatment and then observe its effects on the subjects (subjects in experiments are called experimental units).

Sampling Techniques

A variety of sampling methods can be employed, individually or in combination including but not limited to:

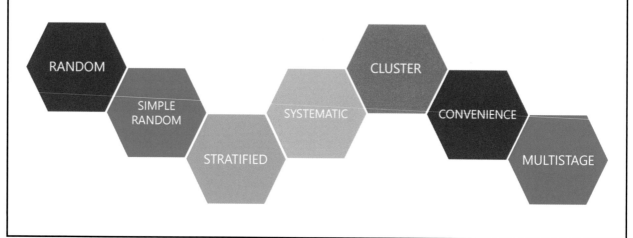

RANDOM

SIMPLE RANDOM

STRATIFIED

SYSTEMATIC

CLUSTER

CONVENIENCE

MULTISTAGE

RANDOM SAMPLE

Members from the population are selected in such a way that each individual member in the population has an equal chance of being selected.

NUMBERS ADDED

HAT

Randomly picks a handful of numbers from the hat.

SIMPLE RANDOM SAMPLE

A sample of *n* subjects is selected in such a way that every possible sample of the same size *n* has the same chance of being chosen.

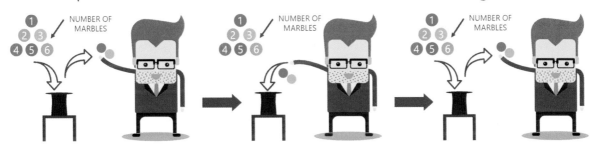

1st pick: randomly picks 2 marbles from the hat containing six different colored marbles.

2nd pick: replaces the marbles back in the hat.

3rd pick: randomly picks 2 marbles from the hat again. The same chance of picking the same colored marbles exists.

STRATIFIED SAMPLING

Subdivide the population into at least two different subgroups that share the same characteristics, then draw a sample from each subgroup (or stratum).

WOMEN   MEN

SYSTEMATIC SAMPLING

Select some starting point and then select every *k*th element in the population.

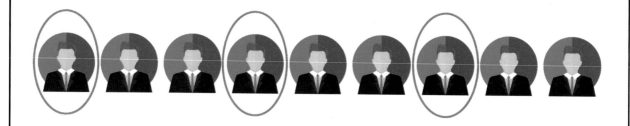

CLUSTER SAMPLING

Divide the population area into sections (or clusters). Then randomly select some of those clusters. Now choose all members from selected clusters.

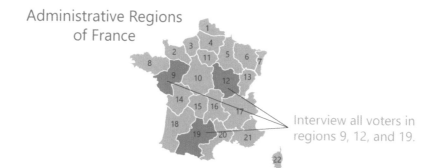

Administrative Regions of France

Interview all voters in regions 9, 12, and 19.

MULTISTAGE SAMPLING

Collect data by using some combination of the basic sampling methods.

In a multistage sample design, pollsters select a sample in different stages, and each stage might use different methods of sampling.

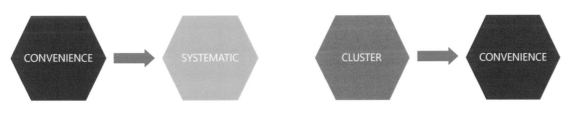

Let's take a survey!

How many miles do you drive to get to LAVC today?

Miles	Frequency (f)
0-4	
5-9	
10-14	
15-19	

Discuss...

(Survey at least 20 people or make up some data. This data will be used in several future sections!)

Which technique(s) are best?

Factors commonly influencing the choice of sampling technique:

Nature and quality of the population

Availability of auxiliary information about units in the population

Measurement requirements (degree of accuracy and/or precision)

Analysis requirements

Cost/operational concerns

Methods of Sampling – Which is best?

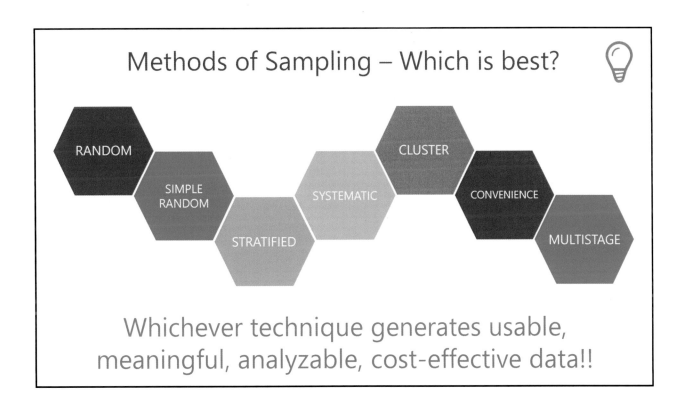

Whichever technique generates usable, meaningful, analyzable, cost-effective data!!

Section 02

2.1 Frequency Distributions for Organizing and Summarizing Data
2.2 Histograms
2.3 Graphs That Enlighten and Graphs That Deceive

Companion to *Elementary Statistics*, Thirteenth Edition and the Triola Stats Series, by Mario F. Triola.

Characteristics of Data

DISTRIBUTION — The nature or shape of the spread of data over the range of values (such as bell-shaped, uniform, or skewed).

CENTER — A representative value that indicates where the middle of the data set is located.

VARIATION — A measure of the amount that the data values vary.

Characteristics of Data (Continued)

OUTLIERS — Sample values that lie very far away from the vast majority of other sample values.

TIME — Changing characteristics of the data over time.

Frequency Distribution Elements

A frequency distribution (sometimes called a frequency table) shows how a data set is partitioned among all of several categories (or classes) by listing all of the categories along with the number (frequency) of data values in each of them.

 (LCL) are the smallest numbers that actually belong to different classes.

 (UCL) are the largest numbers that actually belong to different classes.

Frequency Distribution Elements (Cont.)

CLASS BOUNDARIES — The numbers used to separate classes, but without the gaps created by class limits.

CLASS MIDPOINTS — The values in the middle of the classes and can be found by adding the lower class limit to the upper class limit and dividing the sum by 2.

 The difference between two consecutive frequency distribution elements.

RELATIVE FREQUENCY

The relative frequency is found by dividing the class frequency by the sum of all frequencies.

$$\text{relative frequency} = \frac{\text{class frequency}}{\text{sum of all frequencies}}$$

Relative Frequency Histogram has the same shape and horizontal scale as a histogram, but the vertical scale is marked with relative frequencies instead of actual frequencies.

Frequency Distribution Elements

How many miles did you drive to get to LAVC today?

Miles	Freq. (f)	LCL	UCL	Class Boundaries	Class Midpoint	Class Width	Relative Freq.
0-4							
5-9							
10-14							
15-19							

Use the same survey results from the Section 01...

HISTOGRAM

A visual tool called a histogram is used to analyze the shape of the distribution of the data.

A histogram is a graph consisting of bars of equal width drawn adjacent to each other (unless there are gaps in the data).

The horizontal scale represents the classes of quantitative data values.

The vertical scale of the bars correspond to the frequency values.

Histogram Construction Rules

A histogram is a graph of a frequency distribution.
Rules:

There are no gaps between the bars. (Use the class boundaries.)

The "origin" is never labeled zero.

The axes must be appropriately labeled.

Frequency Histogram

How many miles did you drive to get to LAVC today?

Miles	
0-4	
5-9	
10-14	
15-19	

Use the same survey results from the Section 01...

Why Histograms?

Where can I use a histogram?

What does a histogram show?

How can I use it to make money?

Relative Frequency Histogram

How many miles did you drive to get to LAVC today?

Miles	Freq. (f)	Relative Freq.
0-4		
5-9		
10-14		
15-19		

Use the same survey results from the Section 01...

Frequency Polygon

A frequency polygon is a line segment graph of class midpoints versus frequency. Rules:

The axes must be appropriately labeled.

The next class midpoint (with zero frequency) must be added to the graph on either side.

The resulting graph always looks like "mountains."

The "origin" is never labeled zero.

Frequency Polygon

How many miles did you drive to get to LAVC today?

Miles	Freq. (f)
0-4	
5-9	
10-14	
15-19	

Use the same survey results from the Section 01...

Section 03

3.1 Measures of Center

3.2 Measures of Variation

Companion to *Elementary Statistics*, Thirteenth Edition and the Triola Stats Series, by Mario F. Triola.

Characteristics of Data

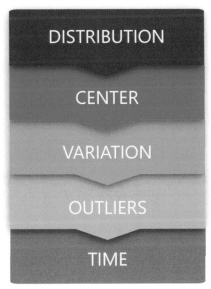

DISTRIBUTION — The nature or shape of the spread of data over the range of values (such as bell-shaped, uniform, or skewed).

CENTER — A representative value that indicates where the middle of the data set is located.

VARIATION — A measure of the amount that the data values vary.

OUTLIERS — Sample values that lie very far away from the vast majority of other sample values.

TIME — Changing characteristics of the data over time.

Notation

 $\sum$ Denotes the sum of a set of values.

 x Is the variable usually used to represent the individual data values.

 n Represents the number of data values in a sample.

 N Represents the number of data values in a population.

ARITHMETIC MEAN

Arithmetic Mean (often shortened to "Mean" and sometimes called "Average") is the measure of center obtained by adding the values and dividing the total by the number of values.

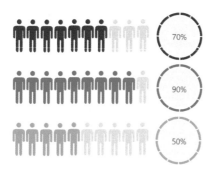

$210\% \div 3$

Arithmetic Mean

$$\bar{x} = \frac{\sum x}{n}$$

SAMPLE MEAN
(pronounced 'x-bar') denotes the mean of a set of sample values.

$$\mu = \frac{\sum x}{N}$$

POPULATION MEAN
(pronounced 'mu') denotes the mean of all values in a population.

Arithmetic Mean

Find the mean peanut count per snack pack. Five randomly sampled snack packs yielded the following peanut counts:

62 peanuts, 62 peanuts, 66 peanuts, 64 peanuts, and 63 peanuts.

Advantages and Disadvantages of Mean

ADVANTAGE	DISADVANTAGE
Sample means drawn from the same population tend to vary less than other measures of center. Takes every data value into account.	Is sensitive to every data value, one extreme value can affect it dramatically. It is not a resistant measure of center.

MEDIAN

Median is the middle value when the original data values are arranged in order of increasing (or decreasing) magnitude.

It is often denoted by $\tilde{x}$ (pronounced 'x-tilde').

It is a resistant measure of the center (Resistant measures are not affected by an extreme value!).

How to Calculate the Median

 Sort the values (arrange them in order).

 If the number of data values is odd, the median is the number located in the exact middle of the list.

 If the number of data values is even, the median is found by computing the mean of the two middle numbers.

Median – Odd Number of Values

Find the median of these numbers:

25.40   21.10   20.42   20.48   20.73   21.10   20.66

Median – Even Number of Values

Find the median of these numbers:

45.40   41.10   40.42   40.73   40.48   41.10

MODE

Mode is the value that occurs with the greatest frequency.

Bimodal data have two data values that occur with the same greatest frequency.

Multimodal data have more than two data values that occur with the same greatest frequency.

Data without a mode—called "no mode"—do not have any repeated data values.

Mode is a Special Measure of Center

Mode is the only measure of central tendency that can be used with nominal data.

Find the Mode:

35.40   31.10   30.42   30.73   30.48   31.10

127   127   127   455   455   455   888   888   899

11   22   33   46   57   68   79   100

Which Measure of Center Should I Use?

Why are there different measures?

Which one should you use with your data/study? Why?

What is our favorite measure of center in this class?

Frequency Distribution Mean

Assume that all sample values in each class are equal to the class midpoint.

Use class midpoint of classes for variable y.

$$\bar{x} = \frac{\sum(fy)}{\sum f} = \frac{\sum(fy)}{n}$$

Frequency Distribution Mean

Calculate the mean miles driven to LAVC.

$$\bar{x} = \frac{\sum(fy)}{\sum f} = \frac{\sum(fy)}{n}$$

Miles	Freq. (f)	Midpoint (y)	fy
0-4			
5-9			
10-14			
15-19			

Use the same survey results from the Section 01...

Measures of Variation

STANDARD DEVIATION — The standard deviation of a set values is a measure of how much data values deviate away from the mean.

VARIANCE — The variance of a set values is a measure equal to the square of the standard deviation.

RANGE — The range of a set of data values is the difference between the maximum data value and the minimum data value.

Standard Deviation

$$s = \sqrt{\frac{\sum (x - \bar{x})^2}{n-1}}$$

$$s = \sqrt{\frac{n\left(\sum x^2\right) - \left(\sum x\right)^2}{n(n-1)}}$$

Sample Standard Deviation denotes the standard deviation of a set of sample values.

$$\sigma = \sqrt{\frac{\sum (x - \mu)^2}{N}}$$

Population Standard Deviation (pronounced 'sigma') denotes the standard deviation of all values in a population.

Important Properties of Standard Deviation

The units of the standard deviation are the same as the units of the original data values.

The standard deviation is a measure of variation of all values from the mean.

The value of the standard deviation is usually positive (it is never negative).

The value of the standard deviation can increase dramatically with the inclusion of one or more outliers (data values far away from all others).

Standard Deviation (Difficult Method)

Find the standard deviation of the peanut count.

62 peanuts, 62 peanuts, 66 peanuts, 64 peanuts, and 63 peanuts

$$s = \sqrt{\frac{\sum (x - \bar{x})^2}{n-1}}$$

Standard Deviation (Shortcut Method)

Find the standard deviation of the peanut count.

62 peanuts, 62 peanuts, 66 peanuts, 64 peanuts, and 63 peanuts

$$s = \sqrt{\frac{n\left(\sum x^2\right) - \left(\sum x\right)^2}{n(n-1)}}$$

Frequency Distribution Standard Deviation

Assume that all sample values in each class are equal to the class midpoint.

Use class midpoint of classes for variable y.

$$s = \sqrt{\frac{n\left[\sum(fy^2)\right] - \left[\sum(fy)\right]^2}{n(n-1)}}$$

Frequency Distribution Standard Deviation

Calculate the standard deviation of miles driven to LAVC.

Miles	Freq. (f)	Midpoint (y)	fy	y^2	fy^2
0-4					
5-9					
10-14					
15-19					

$$s = \sqrt{\frac{n\left[\sum(fy^2)\right] - \left[\sum(fy)\right]^2}{n(n-1)}}$$

Use the same survey results from the Section 01...

Which formula when?

It is unlikely to have entire population data; therefore, it is likely that only formulas for $\bar{x}$ and s will be used in this class.

If the data is a list of actual numbers, use:

$$\bar{x} = \frac{\sum x}{n} \qquad s = \sqrt{\frac{n\left(\sum x^2\right) - \left(\sum x\right)^2}{n(n-1)}}$$

If the data is a frequency distribution of data ranges organized into classes, use:

$$\bar{x} = \frac{\sum(fy)}{\sum f} = \frac{\sum(fy)}{n} \qquad s = \sqrt{\frac{n\left[\sum(fy^2)\right] - \left[\sum(fy)\right]^2}{n(n-1)}}$$

Section 04

3.2 Measures of Variation

3.3 Measures of Relative Standing and Boxplots

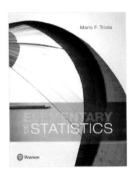 

Companion to *Elementary Statistics*, Thirteenth Edition and the Triola Stats Series, by Mario F. Triola.

Characteristics of Data

DISTRIBUTION — The nature or shape of the spread of data over the range of values (such as bell-shaped, uniform, or skewed).

CENTER — A representative value that indicates where the middle of the data set is located.

VARIATION — A measure of the amount that the data values vary.

OUTLIERS — Sample values that lie very far away from the vast majority of other sample values.

TIME — Changing characteristics of the data over time.

Empirical Rule

For data sets having a distribution that is approximately bell-shaped, the following properties apply:

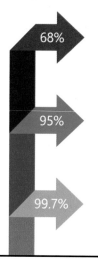

About 68% of all values fall within 1 standard deviation of the mean. The area of the shaded region is about 68%.

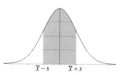

About 95% of all values fall within 2 standard deviations of the mean. The area of the shaded region is about 95%.

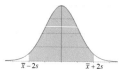

About 99.7% of all values fall within 3 standard deviations of the mean. The area of the shaded region is about 99.7%.

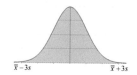

Apply the Empirical Rule

Write three sentences for non-statisticians expressing the empirical rule. Assume that this data is bell-shaped! (WHY?)

Miles	Freq. (f)
0-4	
5-9	
10-14	
15-19	

Use the same survey results from the Section 01...

Chebyshev's Theorem

The proportion (or fraction) of any set of data lying within k standard deviations of the mean is always at least $1-1/k^2$, where k is any positive number greater than 1.

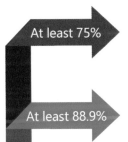

At least 75%

For $k=2$, at least 3/4 (or 75%) of all values lie within 2 standard deviations of the mean.

At least 88.9%

For $k=3$, at least 8/9 (or 88.9%) of all values lie within 3 standard deviations of the mean.

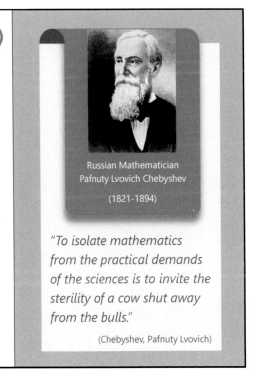

Russian Mathematician
Pafnuty Lvovich Chebyshev

(1821-1894)

"To isolate mathematics from the practical demands of the sciences is to invite the sterility of a cow shut away from the bulls."

(Chebyshev, Pafnuty Lvovich)

Apply Chebyshev's Theorem

Write two sentences for non-statisticians expressing Chebyshev's Theorem. Must the data be bell-shaped?

Miles	Freq. (f)
0-4	
5-9	
10-14	
15-19	

Use the same survey results from the Section 01...

z-score (or standardized value)

z-score (or standardized value) is the number of standard deviations that a given value, x, is above or below the mean.

$$z = \frac{x - \mu}{\sigma}$$
Population z-score

$$z = \frac{x - \bar{x}}{s}$$
Sample z-score

Both formulas yield the same value. The mean and standard deviation are contextual based on information from the sample or the population.

Always round z-scores to two decimal places.

Interpretation of z-scores

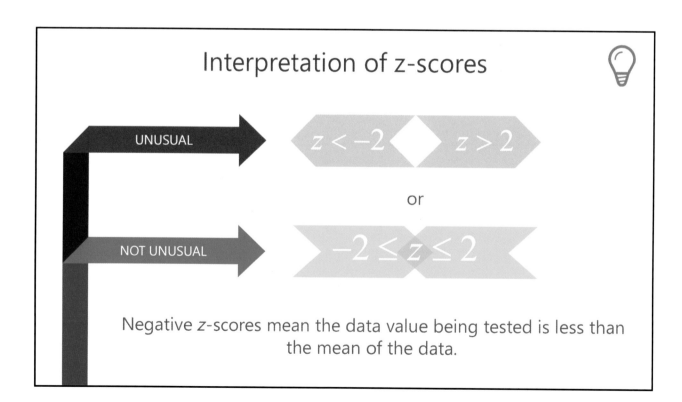

UNUSUAL $\quad z < -2 \quad \diamond \quad z > 2$

or

NOT UNUSUAL $\quad -2 \leq z \leq 2$

Negative z-scores mean the data value being tested is less than the mean of the data.

z-score

Mary runs the mile in 4.3 minutes. Is this mile time unusual if the mean adult female mile time is 5.7 minutes with a standard deviation of 0.73 minutes?

Percentiles

Percentiles are measures of location. There are 99 percentiles denoted $P_1, P_2, \ldots, P_{99}$, which divide a set of data into 100 groups with about 1% of the values in each group.

n total number of values in the data set.

k percentile (whole number from 1-99)

L locator that gives the position of the data set value (ordinal number--1st, 2nd, 3rd, ...)

k^{th} percentile → data value

When supplied with a percentile, use this method to find the data value whose position corresponds to the given percentile.

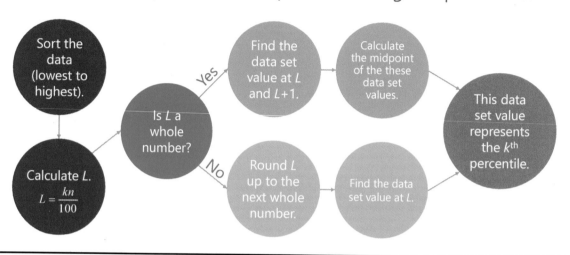

Sort the data (lowest to highest).

Calculate L.
$$L = \frac{kn}{100}$$

Is L a whole number?

Yes → Find the data set value at L and $L+1$. → Calculate the midpoint of the these data set values.

No → Round L up to the next whole number. → Find the data set value at L.

This data set value represents the kth percentile.

---

data value → k^{th} percentile

When supplied with a data value from a list of values in a data set, use this method to find the percentile corresponding to the given data value.

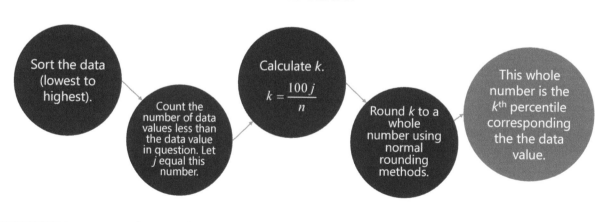

Sort the data (lowest to highest).

Count the number of data values less than the data value in question. Let j equal this number.

Calculate k.
$$k = \frac{100j}{n}$$

Round k to a whole number using normal rounding methods.

This whole number is the kth percentile corresponding the the data value.

Percentile

123 134 135 141 142 144 146 148 151 151 156 166 167

What data value represents the 71st percentile?

144 is what percentile?

Percentile

435   439   439   450   456   467   469   481   481   481   489   499

What data value represents the 25th percentile?

481 is what percentile?

Quartiles (Special Percentiles for Boxplots)

Q_1 FIRST QUARTILE The data set value representing the 25th percentile separating the bottom 25% of the sorted data values from the top 75% of data values.

Q_2 MEDIAN The data set value representing the 50th percentile separating the bottom 50% of the sorted data values from the top 50% of data values. Always calculate this value as the median!

Q_3 THIRD QUARTILE The data set value representing the 75th percentile separating the bottom 75% of the sorted data values from the top 25% of data values.

Boxplot

Boxplots divide sorted data values into four equal percentage parts using Q_1, median (Q_2), and Q_3.

Find the 5-number summary (minimum, Q_1, median (Q_2), Q_3, maximum).

Construct a scale with values that include the minimum and maximum data values.

Construct a box (rectangle) extending from Q_1 to Q_3 and draw a vertical line in the box at the value of median (Q_2).

Draw horizontal lines extending outward from the box to the minimum and maximum values.

Construct a Boxplot

Construct a boxplot for the following data:

8.5   14   71   77   78   89   100   124   136   150

Section 05

4.1 Basic Concepts of Probability

4.2 Addition Rule and Multiplication Rule

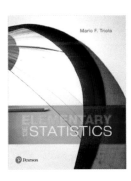

Companion to *Elementary Statistics*, Thirteenth Edition and the Triola Stats Series, by Mario F. Triola.

Probability

PROBABILITY — The study of how likely it is that a given event occurs.

EVENT — Any collection of results or outcomes of a procedure.

SIMPLE EVENT — An outcome or an event that cannot be further broken down into simpler components.

SAMPLE SPACE — All possible simple events.

SAMPLE SIZE — The number of simple events in the sample space.

Notation

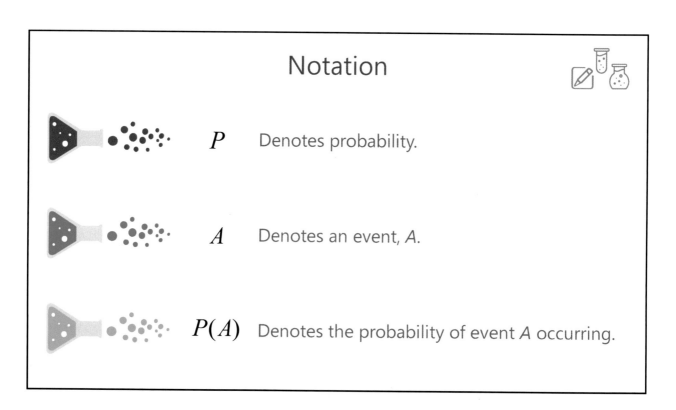

P — Denotes probability.

A — Denotes an event, A.

$P(A)$ — Denotes the probability of event A occurring.

Single, Fair, Six-Sided Dice

Calculate the probability of rolling a 2.

Calculate the probability of rolling an odd number.

Calculate the probability of rolling an even number.

CLASSICAL PROBABILITY

Assume that a given procedure, *A*, has *n* different simple events and that each of those simple events has an equal chance of occurring. If event *A* can occur in *s* of these *n* ways, then

$$P(A) = \frac{s}{n} = \frac{\text{number of ways A can occur}}{\text{number of different simple events}}$$

The classical approach to probability requires equally likely simple events in the sample space.

Testing the dice results...

How would one test the calculated classical probabilities associated with rolling a dice?

What if the results are not as expected? What could be done?

What might be wrong?

RELATIVE FREQUENCY PROBABILITY

Conduct (or observe) a procedure, and count the number of times event *A* actually occurs. Based on these actual results, *P(A)* is approximated as

$$P(A) = \frac{\text{number of times A occurred}}{\text{number of times procedure was repeated}}$$

The relative frequency probability is an approximation of the actual probability.

Dice Rolling Experiment

Roll a single, fair, six-sided dice 75 times. Discuss...

Dice Roll	Frequency	Relative Frequency
1	12	
2	6	
3	13	
4	12	
5	19	
6	13	

More Dice Rolling Experiment

Calculate the relative frequency probability. Discuss...

Dice Roll	Frequency	Relative Frequency
1	204	
2	102	
3	221	
4	204	
5	323	
6	221	

Law of Large Numbers

As a procedure is repeated again and again, the relative frequency probability of an event tends to approach the actual probability.

Note: The Law of Large Numbers only applies when all of the simple events of the experiment are equally likely!!!

Descriptions of Probability Values

CERTAIN — Event *A* occurs every time when the experiment is attempted. $P(A) = 1.00$

LIKELY — Event *A* occurs more often than not when the experiment is attempted. $0.50 < P(A) < 1.00$

50/50 — Event *A* occurs randomly. Event *A* or not *A* are equally likely. $P(A) = 0.50$

UNLIKELY — Event *A* occurs less often than not when the experiment is attempted. $0.00 < P(A) < 0.50$

IMPOSSIBLE — Event *A* never occurs when the experiment is attempted. $P(A) = 0.00$

Descriptions of Events

COMPOUND — Any event combining two or more simple events.

DISJOINT — Events *A* and *B* do not overlap.

MUTUALLY EXCLUSIVE — Events *A* and *B* cannot occur at the same time.

INDEPENDENT — The occurrence of event *A* does not affect the probability of event *B*.

DEPENDENT — The occurrence of event *A* changes the probability of event *B*.

ADDITION RULE

$$P(A \text{ or } B) = P(A) + P(B) - P(A \text{ and } B)$$

where $P(A \text{ and } B) = P$(event *A* and event *B* both occur at the same time as a single outcome of a procedure)

In the addition rule, the word "or" in $P(A \text{ or } B)$ suggests addition. Add $P(A)$ and $P(B)$, being careful to add in such a way that every outcome is counted only once.

MULTIPLICATION RULE

$$P(A \text{ and } B) = P(A) \, P(B|A)$$

where

$P(A \text{ and } B) = P(\text{event } A \text{ occurs first then event } B \text{ occurs second})$

$P(B|A) = P(\text{event } B \text{ occurs after/given event } A \text{ occurs})$

In the multiplication rule, the word "and" in $P(A \text{ and } B)$ suggests multiplication. Multiply $P(A)$ and $P(B)$, but be sure that the probability of event B takes into account the previous occurrence of event A.

 Single, Fair, Six-Sided Dice

Calculate the probability of rolling a 2 or an odd number.

Calculate the probability of rolling a 2 or an even number.

Calculate the probability of rolling a 2 and then an even number.

STANDARD PLAYING CARDS

52 Playing Cards

4 Suits: ♣(Clubs), ♠(Spades), ♥(Hearts), ♦(Diamonds)

13 Values: 2, 3, 4, 5, 6, 7, 8, 9, 10, *J*(Jack), *Q*(Queen), *K*(King), *A*(Ace)

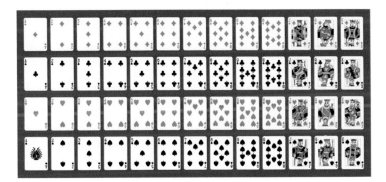

Playing Cards

Calculate the probability of drawing a queen of diamonds.

Calculate the probability of drawing a nine.

Calculate the probability of drawing a club.

Playing Cards

Calculate the probability of drawing an ace or a heart.

Find the probability of drawing a three and then a diamond with replacement.

Find the probability of drawing a spade and then a heart without replacement.

Yahtzee

Calculate the probability of rolling a Yahtzee (five dice with the same value at the same time).

Section 06

4.3 Complements, Conditional Probability, and Bayes' Theorem

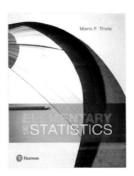 

Companion to *Elementary Statistics*, Thirteenth Edition and the Triola Stats Series, by Mario F. Triola.

PROBABILITY

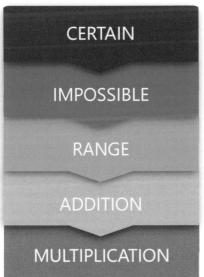

CERTAIN — Event *A* occurs every time when the experiment is attempted. $P(A) = 1.00$

IMPOSSIBLE — Event *A* never occurs when the experiment is attempted. $P(A) = 0.00$

RANGE — For any event *A*, the probability of *A* is between 0.00 and 1.00, inclusive. $0.00 \leq P(A) \leq 1.00$

ADDITION — $P(A \text{ or } B) = P(A) + P(B) - P(A \text{ and } B)$ where $P(A \text{ and } B) = P(A \text{ and } B \text{ at the same time})$

MULTIPLICATION — $P(A \text{ and } B) = P(A)\,P(B|A)$ where $P(A \text{ and } B) = P(A \text{ 1}^{st} \text{ then } B \text{ 2}^{nd})$; $P(B|A) = P(B \text{ given } A)$

More Probability

COMPLEMENT — All outcomes in which the event A does not occur.

AT LEAST — "At least 7" means "7" or "8" or "9" or "10" or …

AT MOST — "At most 4" means "4" or "3" or "2" or "1" or …

MORE THAN — "More than 12" means "13" or "14" or "15" or …

FEWER THAN — "Fewer than 9" means "8" or "7" or "6" or …

Notation

$\overline{A}$ — The complement of event A.

$\geq$ — "At least."

$\leq$ — "At most."

$>$ — "More than."

$<$ — "Fewer than."

Finding and Using Complements

The probability of the complement of *A* is found by calculating the probability of *A* and subtracting that value from 100% (or 1).

$$P(\overline{A}) = 1 - P(A)$$

It is impossible for an event and its complement to occur at the same time.

To find the probability of "at least one" of event *B*, calculate the probability of "none" of event *B* then subtract that result from 1. Note that event *B* must be discrete!

$$P(B \geq 1) = 1 - P(B < 1) \qquad \text{(For any event, B)}$$

$$P(B \geq 1) = 1 - P(B = 0) \qquad \text{(For any discrete event, B)}$$

Venn Diagrams

A Venn diagram shows all possible logical relations between a finite collection of outcomes.

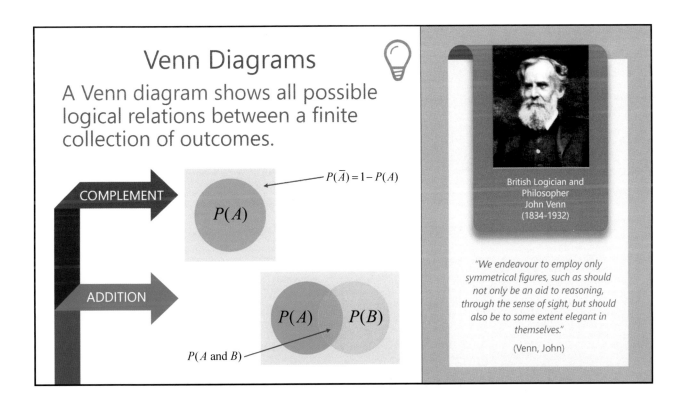

Complements

Calculate the probability of not rolling a 2.

Find the probability of not drawing a four of diamonds.

Find the probability of not drawing a spade.

Complements

Blue Productions supplies Blu-ray discs in lots of 72. Blue Productions know that their Blu-ray discs have a reported defect rate of 0.3%. Find the probability of getting at least one defective disc in a lot of 72?

Probability Types

PRIOR ← EXAMPLE

So far, these are the probabilities that have been calculated in this class.

A prior probability is an initial probability value originally calculated before any additional information is obtained.

The probability of successive events in the multiplication rule is calculated as a single event.

POSTERIOR ← EXAMPLE

After relevant evidence is taken into account, the conditional probability is assigned.

A posterior probability is a probability value that has been revised using additional information that is later obtained.

Bayes' Theorem

CONDITIONAL PROBABILITY

$$P(B \mid A) = \frac{P(A \text{ and } B)}{P(A)}$$

where $P(B \mid A) = P$(event B occurs given that event A has already occurred)

A conditional probability of an event is a probability obtained with the additional information that some other event has already occurred.

Smoking Survey (1 of 3)

Football fans were surveyed about their smoking habits. Two of nine men smoke, and eleven of sixteen women do not smoke.

Organize the smoking survey results in a gender versus smoking status table.

Find the probability of selecting a woman from the survey results.

Smoking Survey (2 of 3)

Find the probability of selecting a non-smoker from the survey results.

Find the probability of selecting a non-smoker who is also a woman from the survey results.

Find the probability of selecting a woman who is also a non-smoker from the survey results.

Smoking Survey (3 of 3)

Find the probability of selecting a non-smoker or a woman from the survey results.

Find the probability of selecting a non-smoker from the survey results given that the subject is a woman.

Find the probability of selecting a woman from the survey results given that the subject is a non-smoker.

Bayes' Theorem

Bayes' Theorem can be used with sequential events, whereby new additional information is obtained for a subsequent event, and the new information is used to revise the probability of the initial event.

Bayes' Theorem is best illustrated with a tree diagram.

All sets of events must be must be disjoint and exhaustive meaning that all possibilities for each event must be listed on the tree diagram.

Initial events branch from the initial node.

Subsequent events branch from each of the initial events forming a distinct node at each initial event with all subsequent events listed for each initial event.

Initial

Subsequent

Subsequent

Subsequent

English Statistician and Presbyterian Minister Thomas Bayes (1701-1761)

"For so far as Mathematics do not make men more sober and rational thinkers, wiser and better men, they are only to be considered an amusement, which not ought to take us off from serious business."

(Bayes, Thomas)

Cigar Smoking Survey Respondents

In Akutan, Alaska, men are 77% of the population. It is also known 11.3% of Akutan males smoke cigars while 2.1% of Akutan non-males smoke cigars. One member of the population is selected at random for a survey involving cell phone carriers.

Find the probability that the selected subject is male.

Find the probability that the selected subject is not male.

Express the cigar smoking data as conditional probabilities.

Cigar Smoking Survey Respondents

Although the subject's identity is unknown, the scent of cigar smoke is detected. Find the probability the selected subject is male.

Airbag Fatalities

Airbags are manufactured by Aces (A), Best (B), and Cool (C) at rates of 57%, 26% and 17%, respectively. Airbags occasionally kill (K) passengers when they deploy in accidents. Airbags made by Aces, Best, and Cool do not kill people at rates of 99%, 96%, and 87%, respectively. One airbag is randomly selected for testing.

Express the airbag manufacturing data as probabilities.

Express the airbag fatality data as probabilities.

Airbag Fatalities

If an airbag kills a passenger, calculate the probability that the airbag was manufactured by Cool.

Section 07

4.4 Counting

Companion to *Elementary Statistics*, Thirteenth Edition and the Triola Stats Series, by Mario F. Triola.

Counting is Challenging!

In many probability problems, the big obstacle is finding the total number of outcomes, and this section presents several methods for finding such numbers without directly listing and counting the possibilities.

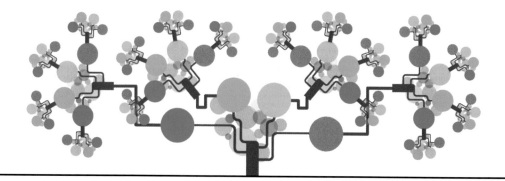

Counting Notation

 n The number of items or possibilities from which to choose.

 r The number of selections or positions.

 $n!$ The factorial symbol denotes the product of decreasing positive whole numbers starting with the number, n, in this case.

MULTIPLICATION RULE

For a sequence of events in which the first event can occur n_1 ways, the second event can occur n_2 ways, the third event can occur n_3 ways, and so on, the total number of outcomes is:

$$n_1 n_2 n_3 \ldots$$

If each event in the sequence occurs in the same number of ways, the total number of outcomes is:

$$n^r$$

Multiplication Rule

How many 4-digit bankcard pin numbers are possible?

A landscaper must plant one flower, one grass, and one tree at each job site. She has 6 different kinds of flowers, 4 different kinds of grasses, and 9 different kinds of trees from which to choose. Find the probability that the job site owner correctly guesses the correct plants on the finished job site.

FACTORIAL RULE

The number of different arrangements (order matters) of n different items when all n of them are selected is:

$n!$

$3! = 6$

Factorial Rule

How many different ways are there to rank 7 horses in a horse race?

If your friend John is traveling to 9 countries in Europe on vacation, what is the probability that you will correctly guess his travel itinerary?

PERMUTATIONS RULE

When *n* different items are available and *r* of them are selected without replacement, the number of different permutations (order counts) is:

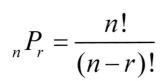

$$_nP_r = \frac{n!}{(n-r)!}$$

$$_5P_2 = 20$$

Permutation Rule

How many different trifectas are possible in a horse race with 12 horses running?

Calculate the probability of winning the exacta in a horse race with 6 horses running?

The number of different permutations (order counts) when n items are available and all n of them are selected without replacement, but n_i of the items are identical to others, is:

$$\frac{n!}{(n_1!)(n_2!)(n_3!)...(n_k!)}$$

$$n = \sum_{i=1}^{k} n_i$$

$$\frac{4!}{(2!)(2!)} = 6$$

Identical Items Rule

How many ordered color combinations are possible if you have 5 red buttons, 2 blue buttons, 6 green buttons, and 3 white buttons?

How many different ways are there to arrange the letters in MATHEMATICS?

COMBINATIONS RULE

When n different items are available and r of them are selected without replacement, the number of different combinations (order does not matter) is:

$$_nC_r = \frac{n!}{r!(n-r)!}$$

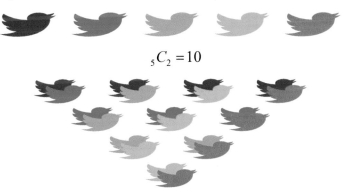

$_5C_2 = 10$

Combinations Rule

From a box of 28 different books, how many different groups of 7 books may be donated to charity?

Find the probability of winning Fantasy Five (a lottery game where the winner correctly chooses five numbered balls (without regard to order) from a group of 39 numbered balls).

Combinations Rule

There are 8 women and 5 men in the math department. What is the probability of choosing a committee of 4 consisting of 3 women and 1 man?

Find the probability of being dealt a royal flush in five-card, no-draw poker.

Section 08

5.1 Probability Distributions

Companion to *Elementary Statistics*, Thirteenth Edition and the Triola Stats Series, by Mario F. Triola.

Statistics Roadmap

CHAP 1	Data and Sampling
CHAP 2-3	Descriptive Statistics and Graphing (what actually did happen)
CHAP 4	Probability
CHAP 5-6	Probability Distributions of Discrete and Continuous Variables (what probably will happen)
CHAP 7-12	Inferential Statistics ("Comparison" of what probably will happen to what actually did happen generating "conclusions" about the data.

Random Variable & Probability Distribution

RANDOM VARIABLE

Random Variable is a variable (typically represented by X) that has a single numerical value, determined by chance, for each outcome of a procedure.

PROBABILITY DISTRIBUTION

A description that maps each value of the random variable to the probability associated with the outcome of the procedure represented by each value of the random variable. They are functions often expressed in the format of a graph, table, or formula.

Craps

Craps is a dice game in which the players make wagers on the outcome of the roll, or a series of rolls, of a pair of dice. Most outcomes depend on the sum of the up faces of two, fair, six-sided dice.

Define the random variable.

Describe the sample space for all possible outcomes of rolling two dice.

Craps Probability Distribution

Determine all possible random variable values and the probability of those outcomes.

Discrete Probability Distribution Requirements

There is a numerical random variable *X* and its values are associated with corresponding probabilities.

The sum of all probabilities must be 1.

$$\sum_X P(X = x) = 1$$

Each probability value must be between 0 and 1 inclusive.

$$0 \le P(X = x) \le 1$$

Craps Probability Distribution

Construct a probability histogram (a relative frequency histogram of probabilities)!

Mean and Standard Deviation of a Probability Distribution

$$\mu = E(X) = \sum_X xP(X = x)$$

Expected Value Mean

$$\sigma = \sqrt{\sum_X \left[(x - \mu)^2 P(X = x) \right]}$$

$$\sigma = \sqrt{\sum_X \left[x^2 P(X = x) \right] - \mu^2}$$

Standard Deviation

Craps Mean and Standard Deviation

Find the mean and standard deviation.

 # Snake Eyes Unusual?

Would it be unusual for a shooter to roll snake eyes?

Roulette Expectation

Roulette is a casino game in which players may choose to place bets on either a single number, a range of numbers, red or black, odd or even, or other outcomes. Consider the amount of money won/lost when betting $5 on 12.

Define the random variable.

Describe the expectation of the random variable in a sentence.

Roulette Expectation

Find the value of winning/losing when betting $5 on 12. The odds paid on a straight bet are 35:1.

Find the probabilities of winning or losing when betting $5 on 12.

Roulette Expectation

Find the expectation of betting $5 on 12.

 Roulette as a Business

How much money should a casino with 5 active roulette tables running 24-hours a day expect to earn based on a LOW average of 45 spins per hour and 25 straight bets in the field per spin?

Section 09

5.2 Binomial Probability Distributions

5.3 Poisson Probability Distributions

Companion to *Elementary Statistics*, Thirteenth Edition and the Triola Stats Series, by Mario F. Triola.

BINOMIAL DISTRIBUTION

A binomial probability distribution results from a procedure that meets all the following requirements:

1. The procedure has a fixed number of trials.
2. The trials must be independent. (The outcome of any individual trial doesn't affect the probabilities in the other trials.)
3. The trials must be mutually exclusive. Each trial must have all outcomes classified into two categories (referred to as success and failure).
4. The probability of a success remains the same in all trials.

Binomial Distribution

 X — The number of successes in n trials (any whole number between 0 and n, inclusive).

 n — The fixed number of trials.

 p — The probability of success in one of the n trials.

 $q = 1 - p$ — The probability of failure in one of the n trials.

Binomial Distribution

 $$P(X = x) = \left({}_{n}C_{x} \right) p^{x} q^{(n-x)}$$ • The probability of getting exactly x successes among the n trials.

 $$\mu = np$$ • The mean of the binomial probability distribution.

 $$\sigma = \sqrt{npq}$$ • The standard deviation of the binomial probability distribution.

Binomial Distribution

 Binomial probability distributions allow us to deal with circumstances in which the outcomes belong to two relevant categories such as acceptable/defective or survived/died.

 Be sure that x and p both refer to the same category being called a success.

 When sampling without replacement, consider events to be independent if $n < 0.05N$.

Widgets (3-pack)

Acme's widgets have a defect rate of 10%. Find the probability that 2 widgets are broken in a 3-pack?

Widgets (15-pack)

Acme's widgets have a defect rate of 10%. Find the probability that 3 widgets are broken in a 15-pack?

Widgets (15-pack)

Acme's widgets have a defect rate of 10%. What is the probability that at least 2 widgets are broken in a 15-pack?

Significantly high/low?

SIGNIFICANTLY HIGH

A random variable value, *X*, is significantly high if the probability of *x* or more successes is 0.05 or less.

$$P(X \geq x) \leq 0.05$$

SIGNIFICANTLY LOW

A random variable value, *X*, is significantly low if the probability of *x* or fewer successes is 0.05 or less.

$$P(X \leq x) \leq 0.05$$

Unusual or Significant... Which Technique?

Significances and unusual are similar concepts. The book says an event is significant if its probability is 0.05 or less. An event is ordinary if its *z*-score is between -2 and 2. The empirical rule states that 95% of the outcomes are ordinary (bell-shaped); therefore, an unusual event occurs less than 5% of the time.

Use the *z*-score on exact/single outcomes. "Is the result unusual?"

Compound outcomes require a probability argument to determine when outcomes are significantly high or low. "Is the result significantly high/low?"

Widgets (15-pack)

Acme's widgets have a defect rate of 10%. Would 2 broken widgets in a 15-pack be significantly high?

Acme's widgets have a defect rate of 10%. Find the mean and standard deviation for the number of widgets that are broken in a 15-pack?

Acme's widgets have a defect rate of 10%. Would it be unusual to purchase a 15-pack containing 1 broken widget?

POISSON DISTRIBUTION

A Poisson probability distribution results from a procedure that meets all the following requirements:

1. The random variable, X, is the number of occurrences of an event over some interval.

2. The occurrences must be random.

3. The occurrences must be independent of each other.

4. The occurrences must be uniformly distributed over the interval being used.

Poisson Distribution

 X — The number of occurrences of some event in an interval (any whole number from 0 to ∞).

 μ — The mean number of occurrences of the event over the interval.

 $e = 2.71828...$ — Euler's number (the base of the natural logarithm).

Swiss Mathematician
Leonhard Euler
(1707-1783)

"Although to penetrate into the intimate mysteries of nature and thence to learn the true causes of phenomena is not allowed to us, nevertheless it can happen that a certain fictive hypothesis may suffice for explaining many phenomena."

(Euler, Leonard)

Poisson Distribution

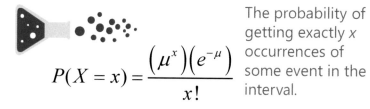 $$P(X = x) = \frac{(\mu^x)(e^{-\mu})}{x!}$$ — The probability of getting exactly x occurrences of some event in the interval.

 μ — The mean of the Poisson distribution.

 $\sigma = \sqrt{\mu}$ — The standard deviation of the Poisson distribution.

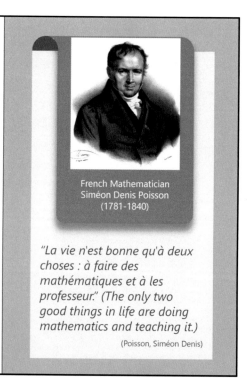

French Mathematician
Siméon Denis Poisson
(1781-1840)

"La vie n'est bonne qu'à deux choses : à faire des mathématiques et à les professeur." (The only two good things in life are doing mathematics and teaching it.)

(Poisson, Siméon Denis)

Poisson Distribution

The Poisson distribution is a discrete probability distribution that applies to occurrences of some event over a specified interval. The interval can be time, distance, area, volume, or some similar unit.

It is often used for describing the behavior of rare events (with small probabilities).

It can also be used to approximate the binomial probability.

Earthquakes Per Day

In one year, 939 worldwide, 5.0+ earthquakes were recorded. Assuming the Poisson distribution, find the mean number of earthquakes per day.

In one year, 939 worldwide, 5.0+ earthquakes were recorded. Assuming the Poisson distribution, what is the probability of exactly 4 worldwide earthquakes with a magnitude of 5.0 or above occurring per day?

Earthquakes Per Day

In one year, 939 worldwide, 5.0+ earthquakes were recorded. Assuming the Poisson distribution, what is the probability of at most 1 worldwide earthquake with a magnitude of 5.0 or above occurring per day?

Earthquakes Per Day

In one year, 939 worldwide, 5.0+ earthquakes were recorded. Assuming the Poisson distribution, would 1 worldwide, 5.0+ earthquake occurring in a day be significantly low?

In one year, 939 worldwide, 5.0+ earthquakes were recorded. Assuming the Poisson distribution, find the standard deviation for the number of earthquakes per day.

In one year, 939 worldwide, 5.0+ earthquakes were recorded. Assuming the Poisson distribution, would it be unusual for 6 worldwide, 5.0+ earthquakes to occur in a day?

Binomial Approximation with Poisson Distribution

When *n* is large, binomial distribution calculations are difficult. The Poisson distribution is sometimes used to approximate the binomial distribution when *n* is large and *p* is small.

Check the following requirements:
$$n \geq 100$$
$$\mu = np \leq 10$$

If both of the requirements are met, then the mean of the binomial distribution may be used for Poisson distribution calculations. The resultant Poisson probability is approximately equal to the difficult-to-calculate binomial probability. $\mu = np$

Look for key words like "approximate" or "estimate" when considering this technique. Be sure to check that the requirements are met!

Widgets (100000-pack)

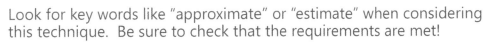
Acme's widgets have a defect rate of 0.01%. Estimate the probability that 26 widgets are broken in a 100000-pack?

Section 10

6.1 The Standard Normal Distribution

6.2 Real Applications of Normal Distributions

Companion to *Elementary Statistics*, Thirteenth Edition and the Triola Stats Series, by Mario F. Triola.

Statistics Roadmap

CHAP 1	Data and Sampling
CHAP 2-3	Descriptive Statistics and Graphing (what actually did happen)
CHAP 4	Probability
CHAP 5-6	Probability Distributions of Discrete and Continuous Variables (what probably will happen)
CHAP 7-12	Inferential Statistics ("Comparison" of what probably will happen to what actually did happen generating "conclusions" about the data.

Random Variable & Probability Distribution

RANDOM WARIABLE	Random Variable is a variable (typically represented by X) that has a single numerical value, determined by chance, for each outcome of a procedure.
PROBABILITY DISTRIBUTION	A description that maps each value of the random variable to the probability associated with the outcome of the procedure represented by each value of the random variable. They are functions often expressed in the format of a graph, table, or formula.
PURPOSE	Probability distributions describe what will probably happen instead of what actually did happen.

Discrete Probability Distribution Requirements

FUNCTION	There is a numerical random variable X and its values are associated with corresponding probabilities.
TOTAL = 100%	The sum of all probabilities must be 1. $$\sum_{X} P(X = x) = 1$$
VALID VALUES	Each probability value must be between 0 and 1 inclusive. $$0 \le P(X = x) \le 1$$

Continuous Probability Distribution Requirements

FUNCTION — There is a numerical continuous random variable X and its values are associated with corresponding probabilities. This function is called a density curve.

TOTAL = 100% — The total area under the curve must equal 1. When working with continuous data, area under the density curve is probability.

VALID VALUES — Every point on the curve must have a vertical height that is 0 or greater. The density curve cannot fall below the horizontal axis.

Normal Distribution

The normal distribution is a continuous probability distribution. As a result, it has a density curve described by a function, $f(x)$.

$$f(x) = \frac{e^{-\frac{1}{2}\left(\frac{x-\mu}{\sigma}\right)^2}}{\sigma\sqrt{2\pi}}$$

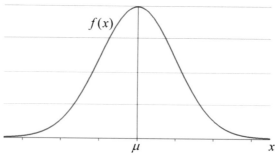

All continuous probability distribution graphs for all sections in this course were created with the tools at http://www.statdistributions.com !

Standard Normal Distribution

The standard normal distribution is a normal probability distribution with $\mu = 0$ and $\sigma = 1$.

The total area under the standard normal distribution's density curve is 1.

Areas under the standard normal distribution curve (which are also probabilities) are found using Table A-2.

Table A-2 is two pages—one page for negative z-scores and the other page for positive z-scores.

Each value in the body of Table A-2 is a cumulative area from the left up to a vertical boundary above a specific z-score.

All z-scores on Table A-2 are two decimal places.

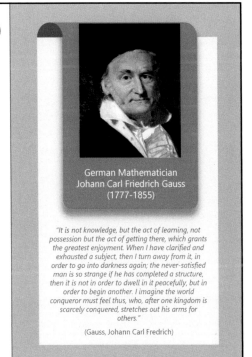

German Mathematician
Johann Carl Friedrich Gauss
(1777-1855)

"It is not knowledge, but the act of learning, not possession but the act of getting there, which grants the greatest enjoyment. When I have clarified and exhausted a subject, then I turn away from it, in order to go into darkness again; the never-satisfied man is so strange if he has completed a structure, then it is not in order to dwell in it peacefully, but in order to begin another. I imagine the world conqueror must feel thus, who, after one kingdom is scarcely conquered, stretches out his arms for others."

(Gauss, Johann Carl Fredrich)

Standard Normal Distribution (Less Than)

Calculate the probability that a randomly selected z-score is less than 1.56.

Standard Normal Distribution (Greater Than)

Calculate the probability that a randomly selected z-score is greater than 2.38.

Standard Normal Distribution (Less Than)

Calculate the probability that a randomly selected z-score is less than -0.76.

Standard Normal Distribution (Greater Than)

Calculate the probability that a randomly selected z-score is greater than -1.11.

Standard Normal Distribution (Between)

Calculate the probability that a randomly selected z-score is between 1.34 and 2.18.

Standard Normal Distribution (Between)

Calculate the probability that a randomly selected z-score is between -2.00 and 2.00.

Standard Normal Distribution (Equal)

Calculate the probability that a randomly selected z-score is equal to -0.59.

Standard Normal Distribution (*p*-value)

Find the z-score of the 75th percentile.

Standard Normal Distribution (*p*-value)

Find the z-score less than 90.5% of z-scores.

z

Non-Standard Normal Distributions

When the mean is not 0 or the standard deviation is not 1, the Standard Normal Distribution Table A-2 cannot be used directly.

The z-score standardizes the normal distribution to the standard normal distribution so that the Table A-2 can be used to find probabilities!

$$z = \frac{x - \mu}{\sigma}$$

Remember to round the z-score to two decimal places in order to use the Table A-2!!

Tall Club International (*p*-value)

Tall Club International has a requirement that women must be at least 70 inches tall. Given that women have normally distributed heights with a mean of 63.7 inches and a standard deviation of 2.9 inches, find the percentage of women who satisfy that height requirement.

Aircraft Cabins (*x*-value)

When designing aircraft cabins, what ceiling height will allow 95% of men to stand without bumping their heads? Men's heights are normally distributed with a mean of 68.6 inches and a standard deviation of 2.8 inches.

Section 11

6.3 Sampling Distributions and Estimators

6.4 The Central Limit Theorem

Companion to *Elementary Statistics*, Thirteenth Edition and the Triola Stats Series, by Mario F. Triola.

PROPORTION

A proportion refers to the fraction of the total that possesses a certain attribute.

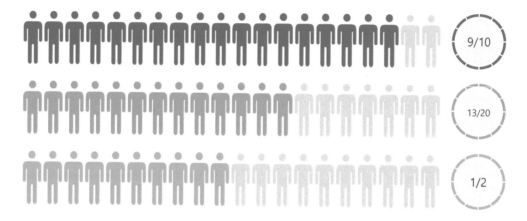

9/10

13/20

1/2

Population Parameters & Sample Statistics

	Population Parameter	Sample Statistic
Mean	μ	$\overline{x}$
Standard Deviation	σ	s
Proportion	p	$\hat{p}$

Mean and Standard Deviation of a Probability Distribution

MEAN

$$\mu = E(X) = \sum_{X} xP(X = x)$$

STANDARD DEVIATION

$$\sigma = \sqrt{\sum_{X}\left[x^2 P(X = x)\right] - \mu^2}$$

 ## Dice Rolling Probability Distribution

Consider rolling a single, fair, six-sided dice. Find the probability distribution, mean, variance, and proportion of odds.

SAMPLING DISTRIBUTION

The sampling distribution of a statistic is the distribution of all values of the statistic when all possible samples of the same size *n* are taken from the same population.

Goal of Sampling Distributions

The mean of the distribution of sample means targets (is approximately equal to) the population mean.

The mean of the distribution of sample variances targets (is approximately equal to) the population variance.

The mean of the distribution of sample proportions targets (is approximately equal to) the population proportion.

Sample means, variances and proportions are unbiased estimators because they target their respective population parameters.

Test Sampling Distribution Targeting

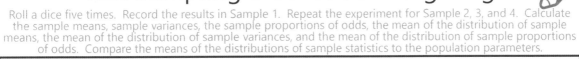

Roll a dice five times. Record the results in Sample 1. Repeat the experiment for Sample 2, 3, and 4. Calculate the sample means, sample variances, the sample proportions of odds, the mean of the distribution of sample means, the mean of the distribution of sample variances, and the mean of the distribution of sample proportions of odds. Compare the means of the distributions of sample statistics to the population parameters.

	Sample 1	Sample 2	Sample 3	Sample 4	Mean of Sample Statistics
$\bar{x}$					
s^2					
$\hat{p}_{odd}$					

Calculations for Sample 1:

$$\bar{x} = \frac{\sum x}{n}$$

$$s^2 = \frac{n\left(\sum x^2\right) - \left(\sum x\right)^2}{n(n-1)}$$

$$\hat{p}_{odd} = \frac{\# \ odd}{n}$$

← Mean of Distribution of Sample Means

← Mean of Distribution of Sample Variances

← Mean of Distribution of Sample Odd Proportions

Purpose of Sampling Distributions?

Do the means of the sample statistics target the population parameters?

Why is this technique so powerful and useful?

What do you predict would happen if there were 10000 samples?

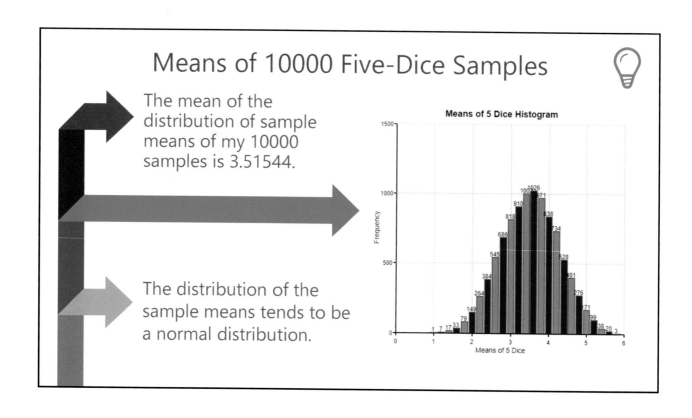

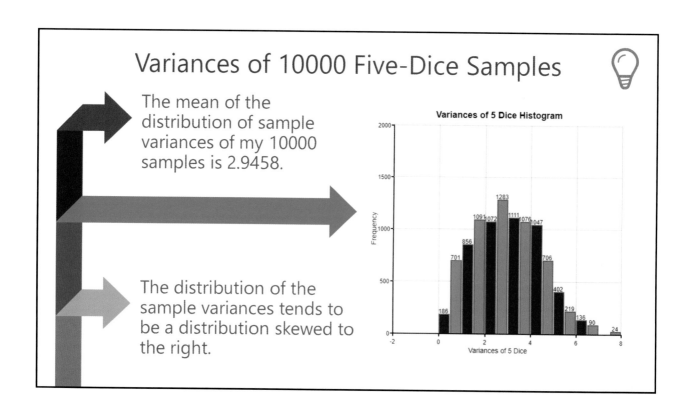

Proportions of Odds of 10000 Five-Dice Samples

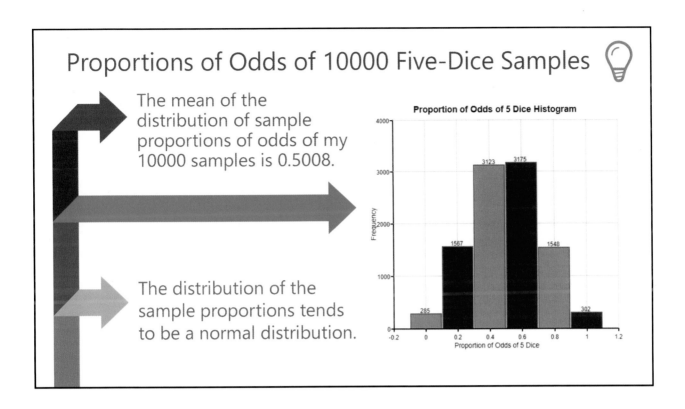

The mean of the distribution of sample proportions of odds of my 10000 samples is 0.5008.

The distribution of the sample proportions tends to be a normal distribution.

Central Limit Theorem (Assumptions)

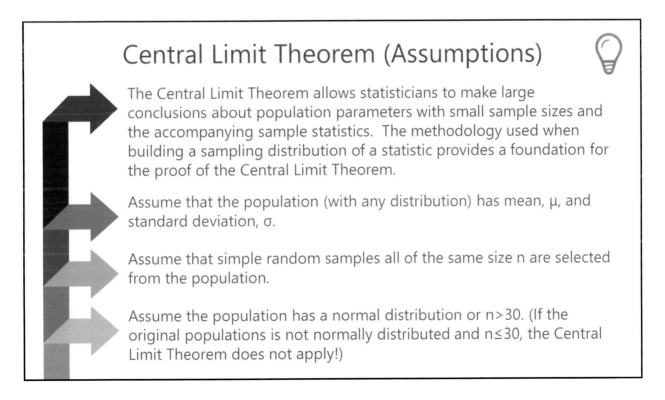

The Central Limit Theorem allows statisticians to make large conclusions about population parameters with small sample sizes and the accompanying sample statistics. The methodology used when building a sampling distribution of a statistic provides a foundation for the proof of the Central Limit Theorem.

Assume that the population (with any distribution) has mean, μ, and standard deviation, σ.

Assume that simple random samples all of the same size n are selected from the population.

Assume the population has a normal distribution or n>30. (If the original populations is not normally distributed and n≤30, the Central Limit Theorem does not apply!)

Central Limit Theorem (Conclusions)

As the sample size, n, increases, the distribution of sample means approaches a normal distribution.

As the sample size, n, increases, the mean of the distribution of sample means approaches the population mean, μ.

$$\mu_{\bar{X}} = \mu$$

As the sample size, n, increases, the standard deviation of the distribution of sample means approaches the population standard deviation, σ, divided by the square root of n.

$$\sigma_{\bar{X}} = \frac{\sigma}{\sqrt{n}}$$

Central Limit Theorem Demonstration

Check out this simulation to see the Central Limit Theorem in action.

http://onlinestatbook.com/stat_sim/sampling_dist/index.html

Central Limit Theorem (Practical Problem Solving)

When working with the mean from a sample, verify that the normal distribution can be used by confirming that the original population has a normal distribution or the sample size is *n>30*.

When working with an individual value from a normally distributed population, use the standard deviation of the population.

$$z = \frac{x - \mu}{\sigma}$$

When working with a mean for some sample of *n* values, use the standard deviation for the distribution of sample means.

$$z = \frac{\overline{x} - \mu_{\overline{x}}}{\sigma_{\overline{x}}} = \frac{\overline{x} - \mu}{\sigma/\sqrt{n}}$$

Elevator Overload (Individual)

An elevator's maximum capacity is 16 passengers or a total weight of 2500 lb. Male weights are normally distributed with a mean of 189 lb. and a standard deviation of 39 lb. Find the probability that 1 randomly selected male has a weight greater than 156.25 lb.

Elevator Overload (Mean of Sample)

An elevator's maximum capacity is 16 passengers or a total weight of 2500 lb. Male weights are normally distributed with a mean of 189 lb. and a standard deviation of 39 lb. Find the probability that a sample of 16 males have a mean weight greater than 156.25 lb. (which exceeds the maximum capacity).

Section 12

6.5 Assessing Normality
6.6 Normal as Approximation to Binomial

Companion to *Elementary Statistics*, Thirteenth Edition and the Triola Stats Series, by Mario F. Triola.

NORMAL QUARTILE PLOT

A normal quartile plot (or normal probability plot) is a graph of points *(x,y)* where each *x*-value is from the original set of sample data, and each *y*-value is the corresponding *z*-score that is expected from the standard normal distribution.

- Normal quartile plots are one way of assessing normality.
- Normal quartile plots are usually generated with technology.
- There are different methods for generating normal quartile plots; therefore, there can be slightly different normal quartile plots for the same data.
- The Ryan-Joiner test includes a normal quartile plot for testing normality.

Normal Quartile Plot Interpretation

The population distribution is probably normal if the points of the normal quartile plot are reasonably close to a straight line and do not have a non-linear, systematic pattern.

The population distribution is not normal if the points of the normal quartile plot are not reasonably close to a straight line or they have a non-linear, systematic pattern.

Note that the Ryan-Joiner test in STATDISK generates a normal quartile plot and also includes a histogram to determine if the data is reasonably bell-shaped.

Normal Quartile Plots (Normal Population)

The following normality assessment was completed with STATDISK. The data was randomly generated from a normal population.

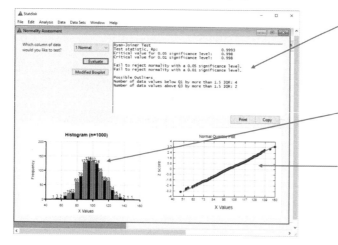

The Ryan-Joiner test concludes with "fail to reject normality" at two significance levels.

The histogram appears bell-shaped.

The normal quartile plot appears to be reasonably close to a straight line without a non-linear, systematic pattern.

Normal Quartile Plots (Uniform Population)

The following normality assessment was completed with STATDISK. The data was randomly generated from a uniform population.

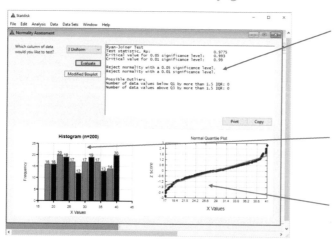

The Ryan-Joiner test concludes with "reject normality" at two significance levels.

The histogram appears uniform.

The normal quartile plot has a non-linear, systematic pattern.

Normal Quartile Plots (Binomial Population)

The following normality assessment was completed with STATDISK. The data was randomly generated from a binomial population.

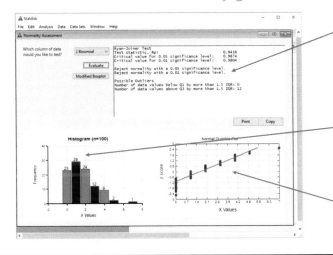

The Ryan-Joiner test concludes with "reject normality" at two significance levels.

The histogram appears skewed to the right.

The normal quartile plot is NOT reasonably close to a straight line .

Normal Quartile Plots (Poisson Population)

The following normality assessment was completed with STATDISK. The data was randomly generated from a Poisson population.

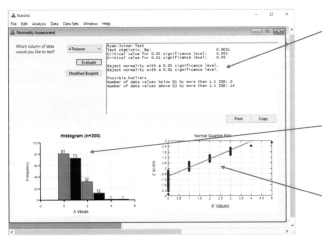

The Ryan-Joiner test concludes with "reject normality" at two significance levels.

The histogram appears skewed to the right.

The normal quartile plot is NOT reasonably close to a straight line .

Binomial Distribution

$$P(X = x) = \left({}_nC_x \right) p^x q^{(n-x)}$$

The probability of getting exactly x successes among the n trials.

$$\mu = np$$

The mean of the binomial probability distribution.

$$\sigma = \sqrt{npq}$$

The standard deviation of the binomial probability distribution.

Poisson Distribution

$$P(X = x) = \frac{\left(\mu^x \right)\left(e^{-\mu} \right)}{x!}$$

The probability of getting exactly x successes among the n trials.

$$\mu$$

The mean of the binomial probability distribution.

$$\sigma = \sqrt{\mu}$$

The standard deviation of the binomial probability distribution.

z-score (or standardized value)

Z-SCORE (OR STANDARDIZED VALUE)
$z = \dfrac{x - \mu}{\sigma}$
UNUSUAL
NOT UNUSUAL
IS THE RESULT UNUSUAL?

z-score (or standardized value) is the number of standard deviations that a given value, x, is above or below the mean.

Always round z-scores to two decimal places.

$z < -2$ $z > 2$

$-2 \leq z \leq 2$

Use the z-score on exact/single outcomes.

Significantly High/Low

SIGNIFICANTLY HIGH
SIGNIFICANTLY LOW
IS THE RESULT SIGNIFICANTLY HIGH/LOW?

A random variable value, X, is significantly high if the probability of x or more successes is 0.05 or less.

$$P(X \geq x) \leq 0.05$$

A random variable value, X, is significantly low if the probability of x or fewer successes is 0.05 or less.

$$P(X \leq x) \leq 0.05$$

Compound outcomes require a probability argument to determine when outcomes are significantly high or low.

Binomial Approximation with Poisson Distribution

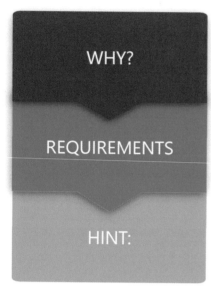

WHY?

REQUIREMENTS

HINT:

When n is large, binomial distribution calculations are difficult. The Poisson distribution is sometimes used to approximate the binomial distribution when n is large and p is small.

$$n \geq 100 \qquad \mu = np \leq 10$$

If both of the requirements are met, then the mean of the binomial distribution may be used for Poisson distribution calculations. $\mu = np$

Look for key words like "approximate" or "estimate" when considering this technique. Be sure to check that the requirements are met!

Binomial Approximation with Normal Distribution

When *n* is large, binomial distribution calculations are difficult. The Normal distribution is sometimes used to approximate the binomial distribution when *np* and *nq* are large.

Check the following requirements: $np \geq 5 \quad nq \geq 5$

If both of the requirements are met, then the mean and standard deviation of the binomial distribution may be used for Normal distribution calculations.

Remember to transform the normal distribution to a *z*-score before using Table A-2.

$$\mu = np \quad \sigma = \sqrt{npq}$$

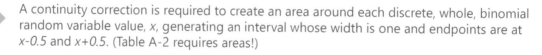

A continuity correction is required to create an area around each discrete, whole, binomial random variable value, *x*, generating an interval whose width is one and endpoints are at *x-0.5* and *x+0.5*. (Table A-2 requires areas!)

Look for key words like "approximate" or "estimate" when considering this technique. Be sure to check that the requirements are met!

Widgets (12-pack)

Acme's widgets have a defect rate of 3%. Find the probability that 4 widgets are broken in a 12-pack?

Widgets (12-pack)

Acme's widgets have a defect rate of 3%. What is the probability that more than 2 widgets are broken in a 12-pack?

Widgets (12-pack)

Acme's widgets have a defect rate of 3%. Would 3 broken widgets in a 12-pack be significantly high?

Acme's widgets have a defect rate of 3%. Find the mean and standard deviation for the number of widgets that are broken in a 12-pack?

Acme's widgets have a defect rate of 3%. Would it be unusual to purchase a 12-pack containing 3 broken widgets?

Widgets (200-pack)

Acme's widgets have a defect rate of 3%. When dealing with a 200-pack, may probabilities for the number of broken widgets be approximated/estimated using the Poisson Distribution? Why, or why not?

Acme's widgets have a defect rate of 3%. When dealing with a 200-pack, may probabilities for the number of broken widgets be approximated/estimated using the Normal Distribution? Why, or why not?

Acme's widgets have a defect rate of 3%. Find the mean and standard deviation for the number of widgets that are broken in a 200-pack?

Widgets (200-pack) (Binomial Distribution)

Acme's widgets have a defect rate of 3%. Find the probability that 8 widgets are broken in a 200-pack using the Binomial Distribution.

Widgets (200-pack) (Poisson Approximation)

Acme's widgets have a defect rate of 3%. Approximate/estimate the probability that 8 widgets are broken in a 200-pack using the Poisson Distribution.

Widgets (200-pack) (Normal Approximation)

Acme's widgets have a defect rate of 3%. Approximate/estimate the probability that 8 widgets are broken in a 200-pack using the Normal Distribution.

Widgets (400-pack)

Acme's widgets have a defect rate of 3%. When dealing with a 400-pack, may probabilities for the number of broken widgets be approximated/estimated using the Poisson Distribution? Why, or why not?

Acme's widgets have a defect rate of 3%. When dealing with a 400-pack, may probabilities for the number of broken widgets be approximated/estimated using the Normal Distribution? Why, or why not?

Acme's widgets have a defect rate of 3%. Find the mean and standard deviation for the number of widgets that are broken in a 400-pack?

Widgets (400-pack) (Normal Approximation)

Acme's widgets have a defect rate of 3%. Approximate/estimate the probability that between 5 and 18 widgets are broken in a 400-pack.

Section 13

7.1 Estimating a Population Proportion

7.2 Estimating a Population Mean

Companion to *Elementary Statistics*, Thirteenth Edition and the Triola Stats Series, by Mario F. Triola.

Statistics Roadmap

CHAP 1	Data and Sampling
CHAP 2-3	Descriptive Statistics and Graphing (what actually did happen)
CHAP 4	Probability
CHAP 5-6	Probability Distributions of Discrete and Continuous Variables (what probably will happen)
CHAP 7-12	Inferential Statistics ("Comparison" of what probably will happen to what actually did happen generating "conclusions" about the data.

Population Parameters & Sample Statistics

	Population Parameter	Sample Statistic
Mean	μ	$\overline{x}$
Standard Deviation	σ	s
Proportion	p	$\hat{p}$

Confidence Intervals

POINT ESTIMATE

A point estimate is a single value (or point) used to approximate a population parameter.

CONFIDENCE INTERVAL

A confidence interval (or interval estimate) is a range (or an interval) of values used to estimate the true value of a population parameter. Graphically, confidence intervals always have two tails.

CONFIDENCE LEVEL

A confidence level is the probability, $1-\alpha$, that the confidence interval actually does contain the population parameter, assuming that the estimation process is repeated a large number of times. (The confidence level is also called degree of confidence, or the confidence coefficient.)

CRITICAL VALUE

A critical value is the number on the borderline separating sample statics that are significantly high or low from those that are not significant.

The number $z_{\alpha/2}$ is an example of a critical value. The z indicates that the z-score value is associated with the standard normal distribution, Table A-2. The $\alpha/2$ indicates that the value of $z_{\alpha/2}$ is at the border separating an area of $\alpha/2$ in the right tail from the rest of the area on the left, $1-\alpha/2$.

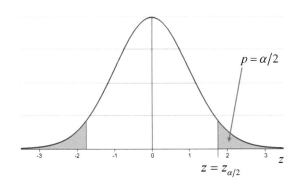

$p = \alpha/2$

$z = z_{\alpha/2}$

MARGIN OF ERROR, *E*

When data from a simple random sample are used to estimate a population parameter, the difference between the sample statistic and the population parameter is an error. The maximum likely amount of that error is the margin of error, denoted by *E*. (The margin of error is also called maximum error of the estimate.)

Confidence Intervals for Estimating One Population Parameter

Population Parameter	Conditions	Confidence Interval	Distribution	Degrees of Freedom (*df*)
Mean, μ	• Simple Random Sample • Normally distributed population and/or $n>30$	$P(\bar{x} - E < \mu < \bar{x} + E) = 1 - \alpha$ $E = t_{\alpha/2} \dfrac{s}{\sqrt{n}}$	Student *t*, Table A-3	$n-1$
	• Simple Random Sample • Normally distributed population and/or $n>30$ • σ is known	$P(\bar{x} - E < \mu < \bar{x} + E) = 1 - \alpha$ $E = z_{\alpha/2} \dfrac{\sigma}{\sqrt{n}}$	Standard Normal *z*, Table A-2	
Standard Deviation, σ	• Simple Random Sample • Normally distributed population	$P\left(\sqrt{\dfrac{(n-1)s^2}{\chi_R^2}} < \sigma < \sqrt{\dfrac{(n-1)s^2}{\chi_L^2}} \right) = 1 - \alpha$	Chi-square, χ^2 Table A-4	$n-1$
Proportion, p	• Simple Random Sample • Binomial Distribution Conditions • $n\hat{p} \geq 5$ and $n\hat{q} \geq 5$	$P(\hat{p} - E < p < \hat{p} + E) = 1 - \alpha$ $E = z_{\alpha/2} \sqrt{\dfrac{\hat{p}\hat{q}}{n}}$	Standard Normal *z*, Table A-2	

Finding the Sample Size Required to Estimate a Population Parameter

Population Parameter	Conditions	Sample size, n, must be at least (always round up!)...
Mean, μ	• Simple Random Sample	$n = \left[\dfrac{(z_{\alpha/2})\sigma}{E} \right]^2$
Standard Deviation, σ	• Simple Random Sample	See Table on the next slide.
Proportion, p	• Simple Random Sample • An estimate for $\hat{p}$ is known.	$n = \dfrac{(z_{\alpha/2})^2 \, \hat{p}\hat{q}}{E^2}$
	• Simple Random Sample	$n = \dfrac{(z_{\alpha/2})^2 \, 0.25}{E^2}$

Sample Size Required to Estimate a Population Standard Deviation

<u>EXAMPLE</u>: For s to be within 20% of σ, and to be 99% confident of that statement, the sample size, n, should be at least 85.

This is equivalent to being 99% confident that:

$$s \in [\sigma - 0.20\sigma, \sigma + 0.20\sigma]$$
$$s \in [0.80\sigma, 1.20\sigma]$$

For s to be within ... of σ,	and to be 95% confident of that statement,	and to be 99% confident of that statement,
	the sample size, n, should be at least...	
1%	19205	33218
5%	768	1336
10%	192	336
20%	48	85
30%	21	38
40%	12	22
50%	8	14

Instagram Awareness (Proportion CI)

The Pew Research Center conducted a survey of 897 adults and found that 76% of them are aware of Instagram. Construct a 93% confidence interval estimate of the proportion of adults who are aware of Instagram.

Instagram Awareness (n for Proportion, $\hat{p}$ known)

The Pew Research Center wishes to estimate the proportion of adults who are aware of Instagram. Assume that a recent Instagram publication indicates that 69% of adults are aware of Instagram. How many adults must the marketing firm randomly survey if they want to be 90% confident that the proportion of adults who are aware of Instagram is within 2% of the true proportion of adults who are aware of Instagram?

Instagram Awareness (*n* for Proportion)

The Pew Research Center wishes to estimate the proportion of adults who are aware of Instagram. How many adults must the marketing firm randomly survey if they want to be 96% confident that the proportion of adults who are aware of Instagram is within 3% of the true proportion of adults who are aware of Instagram?

College Student Ages (Mean CI, σ known)

The mean age of a sample of 40 college students is 23.95 with a standard deviation of 2.55. Assume that prior studies indicate that the standard deviation of college students ages is 2.04. Construct a 99% confidence interval estimate of the mean age of all college students.

Section 14

7.2 Estimating a Population Mean

7.3 Estimating a Population Standard Deviation or Variance

Companion to *Elementary Statistics*, Thirteenth Edition and the Triola Stats Series, by Mario F. Triola.

Population Parameters & Sample Statistics

	Population Parameter	Sample Statistic
Mean	μ	$\overline{x}$
Standard Deviation	σ	s
Proportion	p	$\hat{p}$

Confidence Intervals for Estimating One Population Parameter

Population Parameter	Conditions	Confidence Interval	Distribution	Degrees of Freedom (*df*)
Mean, μ	• Simple Random Sample • Normally distributed population and/or $n>30$	$P(\bar{x}-E<\mu<\bar{x}+E)=1-\alpha$ $E=t_{\alpha/2}\dfrac{s}{\sqrt{n}}$	Student t, Table A-3	$n-1$
	• Simple Random Sample • Normally distributed population and/or $n>30$ • σ is known	$P(\bar{x}-E<\mu<\bar{x}+E)=1-\alpha$ $E=z_{\alpha/2}\dfrac{\sigma}{\sqrt{n}}$	Standard Normal z, Table A-2	
Standard Deviation, σ	• Simple Random Sample • Normally distributed population	$P\left(\sqrt{\dfrac{(n-1)s^2}{\chi_R^2}}<\sigma<\sqrt{\dfrac{(n-1)s^2}{\chi_L^2}}\right)=1-\alpha$	Chi-square, χ^2 Table A-4	$n-1$
Proportion, p	• Simple Random Sample • Binomial Distribution Conditions • $n\hat{p}\geq 5$ and $n\hat{q}\geq 5$	$P(\hat{p}-E<p<\hat{p}+E)=1-\alpha$ $E=z_{\alpha/2}\sqrt{\dfrac{\hat{p}\hat{q}}{n}}$	Standard Normal z, Table A-2	

Finding the Sample Size Required to Estimate a Population Parameter

Population Parameter	Conditions	Sample size, n, must be at least (always round up!)...
Mean, μ	• Simple Random Sample	$n=\left[\dfrac{\left(z_{\alpha/2}\right)\sigma}{E}\right]^2$
Standard Deviation, σ	• Simple Random Sample	See Table on the next slide.
Proportion, p	• Simple Random Sample • An estimate for $\hat{p}$ is known.	$n=\dfrac{\left(z_{\alpha/2}\right)^2\hat{p}\hat{q}}{E^2}$
	• Simple Random Sample	$n=\dfrac{\left(z_{\alpha/2}\right)^2 0.25}{E^2}$

Sample Size Required to Estimate a Population Standard Deviation

EXAMPLE: For *s* to be within 20% of σ, and to be 99% confident of that statement, the sample size, *n*, should be at least 85.

This is equivalent to being 99% confident that:

$$s \in [\sigma - 0.20\sigma, \sigma + 0.20\sigma]$$

$$s \in [0.80\sigma, 1.20\sigma]$$

For *s* to be within ... of σ,	and to be 95% confident of that statement,	and to be 99% confident of that statement,
	the sample size, *n*, should be at least...	
1%	19205	33218
5%	768	1336
10%	192	336
20%	48	85
30%	21	38
40%	12	22
50%	8	14

DEGREES OF FREEDOM, *df*

In general, the number of degrees of freedom, *df*, for a collection of data is the number of values that can vary after at least one restriction is imposed on the whole collection of data. For example, if a data set of 12 numbers is found to have a sum of 250, it is possible to freely assign any numerical value to 11 of those numbers. Since the sum of all 12 numbers is 250, the 12th value cannot be freely assigned because it must be the exact, correct value to force the sum of all 12 numbers to be 250. This means that the sum of a data set of 12 numbers has 11 degrees of freedom.

Student *t* Distribution

The Student *t* distribution is a continuous probability distribution designed to extend statistics beyond the requirement of "large" samples ($n > 30$).

The Student *t* distribution is different for different sample sizes. The sample size determines the number of degrees of freedom, *df*.

The Student *t* distribution has the same, general, symmetric, bell shape as the standard normal distribution but it reflects the greater variability (with wider distributions) that is expected with small samples.

The Student *t* distribution has a mean of $t=0$ (just as the standard normal distribution has a mean of $z=0$).

The standard deviation of the Student *t* distribution varies with the sample size and is greater than one (unlike the standard normal distribution, which has $\sigma=1$).

Use Table A-3 to find critical values for the Student *t* distribution.

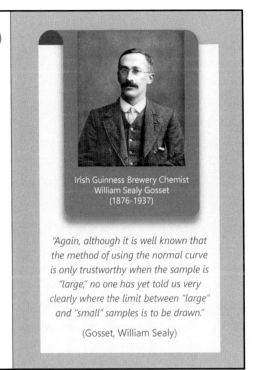

Irish Guinness Brewery Chemist
William Sealy Gosset
(1876-1937)

"Again, although it is well known that the method of using the normal curve is only trustworthy when the sample is "large," no one has yet told us very clearly where the limit between "large" and "small" samples is to be drawn."

(Gosset, William Sealy)

Student *t* Distribution (Graphically)

As the number of degrees of freedom increases, the Student *t* distribution becomes tighter and closer to the standard normal distribution.

As the sample size decreases, the critical values grow larger effectively widening confidence intervals for smaller sample sizes!

Student *t* Distribution at a confidence level of 0.80 for 1, 2, 5, 30, and 10000 degrees of freedom.

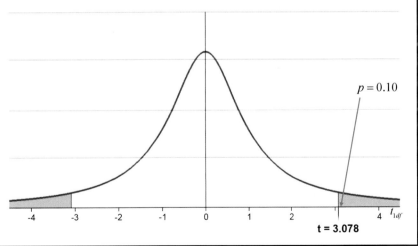

$p = 0.10$

$t = 3.078$

Chi-square Distribution

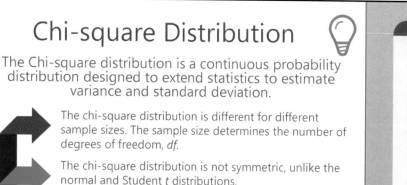

The Chi-square distribution is a continuous probability distribution designed to extend statistics to estimate variance and standard deviation.

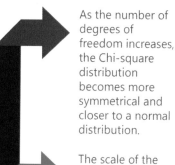

The chi-square distribution is different for different sample sizes. The sample size determines the number of degrees of freedom, *df*.

The chi-square distribution is not symmetric, unlike the normal and Student *t* distributions.

The values of chi-square can be zero or positive, but it cannot be negative.

As the number of degrees of freedom increases, the distribution becomes more symmetric.

Use Table A-4 to find critical values for the Chi-square distribution.

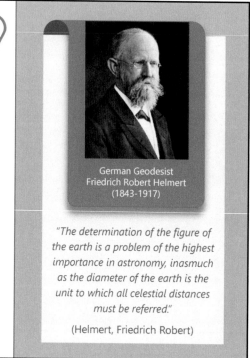

German Geodesist
Friedrich Robert Helmert
(1843-1917)

"The determination of the figure of the earth is a problem of the highest importance in astronomy, inasmuch as the diameter of the earth is the unit to which all celestial distances must be referred."

(Helmert, Friedrich Robert)

Chi-square Distribution (Graphically)

As the number of degrees of freedom increases, the Chi-square distribution becomes more symmetrical and closer to a normal distribution.

The scale of the graphs change because the mean of the Chi-square distribution is not the same for each degree of freedom.

Chi-square Distribution at a confidence level of 0.90 for 4, 12, 40, and 100 degrees of freedom.

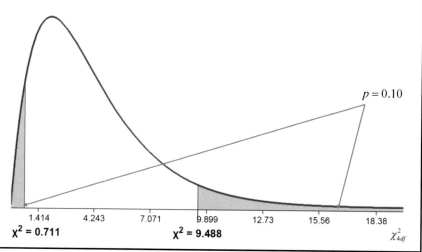

$p = 0.10$

1.414   4.243   7.071   9.899   12.73   15.56   18.38

$\chi^2 = 0.711$ $\chi^2 = 9.488$

χ^2_{4df}

College Student Ages (*n* for Mean)

A marketing firm wishes to estimate the mean age of college students. Assume that prior studies indicate that the standard deviation of college students ages is 2.04. How many students must the marketing firm randomly survey if they want to be 92% confident that the sample mean age of college students is within 0.33 years of the true population mean?

College Student Ages (Mean CI, σ not known)

The mean age of a sample of 40 college students is 23.95 with a standard deviation of 2.55. Construct a 98% confidence interval estimate of the mean age of all college students.

College Student Ages (Standard Deviation CI)

The mean age of a sample of 40 college students is 23.95 with a standard deviation of 2.55. Construct a 95% confidence interval estimate of the standard deviation of the age of all college students.

College Student Ages (*n* for Standard Deviation)

A marketing firm wishes to estimate the standard deviation of the ages of college students. How many students must the marketing firm randomly survey if they want to be 99% confident that the sample standard deviation of the ages of college students is within 5% of the true population standard deviation of ages of college students?

Section 15

8.1 Basics of Hypothesis Testing

8.2 Testing a Claim About Proportion

Companion to *Elementary Statistics*, Thirteenth Edition and the Triola Stats Series, by Mario F. Triola.

Hypotheses

HYPOTHESIS	A hypothesis is a claim or statement about a property of a population.
HYPOTHESIS TEST	A hypothesis test (or test of significance) is a procedure for testing a claim about a property of a population.
NULL HYPOTHESIS, H_0	The null hypothesis, H_0, is a statement about the value of a population parameter that contains equality (= or ≤ or ≥ or special words in later chapters) to some claimed value.
ALTERNATIVE HYPOTHESIS, H_1	The alternative hypothesis, H_1 or H_a or H_A, is a the statement about the value of the population parameter that is true when the null hypothesis is false (≠ or > or < or special words in later chapters).

Hypotheses

The null hypothesis includes the working assumption for the purposes of conducting the hypothesis test. The assumed value of the population parameters will be used in calculating the test statistic.

The alternative hypothesis is usually a new paradigm of thought or understanding being challenged by the hypothesis test.

H_0 and H_1 are complementary.

This book, almost all other books, and almost all professional journals express H_0 using only equality (=). Although this practice is commonly accepted (and will be in this course as well), it undermines the proof-by-contradiction, logical foundation of hypothesis testing.

Testing Criteria

SIGNIFICANCE LEVEL, α

The significance level, α, for a hypothesis test is the probability value used as the cutoff for determining when the sample evidence constitutes significant evidence against the null hypothesis.

CRITICAL REGION

The critical region (or rejection region) is the area corresponding to all values of the test statistic that cause us to reject the null hypothesis.

CRITICAL VALUE

A critical value is any value that separates the critical region (where we reject the null hypothesis) from the values of the test statistic that do not lead to rejection of the null hypothesis.

Testing Criteria

The significance level is the probability of mistakenly rejecting the null hypothesis when it is true. The significance level is set based upon the seriousness of this error BEFORE testing commences.

H_1 describes the critical region. Assuming that the population variable(s) are on the left side of the inequality in H_1, ≠ means two-tailed critical region, > means right-tailed critical region, < means left-tailed critical region.

The significance level is the total area of the critical region. If the critical region is two-tailed, half of the significance level is in one tail, half is in the other tail.

Decision Making

TEST STATISTIC
The test statistic is a value used in making a decision about the null hypothesis, and is found by converting the sample statistic to a score with the assumption that the null hypothesis is true.

p-VALUE, p
The p-value, p, is the probability of getting a value of the test statistic that is at least as extreme as the test statistic obtained from the sample data, assuming that the null hypothesis is true.

Decision Making

A test statistic is a measure of how unusual it would be to obtain the sample data from the experiment if the null hypothesis were true.

If the test statistic is in the critical region, reject H_0.
If the test statistic is not in the critical region, fail to reject H_0.

The p-value, p, is the area of the region having the same shape (same tails) as the critical region with edges formed by the test statistic, not the critical value. For two-tailed tests, the p-value is twice the area of one tail.

If $p \le \alpha$, reject H_0.
If $p > \alpha$, fail to reject H_0.

US Justice System

John is accused of a crime, arrested, and stands trial. The government wishes to test the claim that John is guilty.

Null Hypothesis, H_0: John is innocent.

Alternative Hypothesis, H_1: John is guilty.

Hypothesis test: The trial.

Test statistic: The evidence.

Significance Level: Beyond a reasonable doubt.

The Trial	True State of Nature	
	Null Hypothesis, H_0	Alternative Hypothesis, H_1
	John is innocent.	John is guilty.
Reject H_0 John is guilty beyond a reasonable doubt.	Type I Error, α: Rejecting the null hypothesis when it is actually true.	Correct.
Fail to Reject H_0 John is not guilty.	Correct.	Type II Error, β: Failing to reject the null hypothesis when it is actually false.

Preliminary Conclusions

Circumnavigate the Globe

Phil is a sailor in the year 600 CE who wishes to test the claim that the world is round.

Null Hypothesis, H_0: The world is flat.

Alternative Hypothesis, H_1: The world is round.

Hypothesis test: The journey attempting to circumnavigate the globe.

Test statistic: The curvature or edge of the earth.

Significance Level: To a virtual certainty.

The Trial		True State of Nature	
		Null Hypothesis, H_0	Alternative Hypothesis, H_1
		The world is flat.	The world is round.
Preliminary Conclusions	Reject H_0 The world is round to a virtual certainty.	Type I Error, α: Rejecting the null hypothesis when it is actually true.	Correct.
	Fail to Reject H_0 The world is not round.	Correct.	Type II Error, β: Failing to reject the null hypothesis when it is actually false.

Test Statistics for Testing One Population Parameter

Population Parameter	Conditions	Test Statistic	Distribution	Degrees of Freedom (df)	p-value
Mean, μ	• Simple Random Sample • Normally distributed population and/or $n>30$	$t = \dfrac{\bar{x} - \mu}{\frac{s}{\sqrt{n}}}$	Student t, Table A-3	$n-1$	Use technology or find high and low bounds for p from table.
	• Simple Random Sample • Normally distributed population and/or $n>30$ • σ is known	$z = \dfrac{\bar{x} - \mu}{\frac{\sigma}{\sqrt{n}}}$	Standard Normal z, Table A-2		Found on table.
Standard Deviation, σ	• Simple Random Sample • Normally distributed population	$\chi^2 = \dfrac{(n-1)s^2}{\sigma^2}$	Chi-square, χ^2 Table A-4	$n-1$	Use technology or find high and low bounds for p from table.
Proportion, p	• Simple Random Sample • Binomial Distribution Conditions • $n\hat{p} \geq 5$ and $n\hat{q} \geq 5$	$z = \dfrac{\hat{p} - p}{\sqrt{\frac{pq}{n}}}$	Standard Normal z, Table A-2		Found on table.

Final Words

It is very difficult to formulate the words of the final conclusion. ALWAYS consult this flowchart to determine the correct wording.

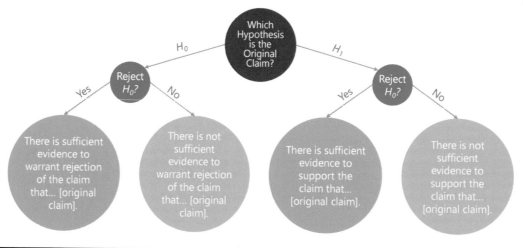

Critical Value Method (8-steps)

1. Extract Information: Read. Read again. Read every single word including the small ones. Determine the population parameter being tested. Extract numerical information and assumptions from the problem. Assign statistics letters to the numbers from the problem. Determine the formula for the test statistic. Transfer the formula for the test statistic to the "test statistic" step. Do not calculate the value of the test statistic until reaching that step.

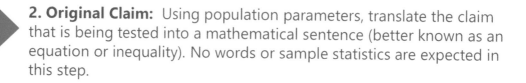

2. Original Claim: Using population parameters, translate the claim that is being tested into a mathematical sentence (better known as an equation or inequality). No words or sample statistics are expected in this step.

Critical Value Method (8-steps)

3. Null Hypothesis, H_0, and Alternative Hypothesis, H_1: Transfer the original claim to either H_0 or H_1. The original claim—exactly as stated in the "original claim" step—must appear in either H_0 or H_1. Remember which mathematical sentences fit with H_0 (eg. $=$, $\leq$, $\geq$) and H_1 (eg. $\neq$, $>$, $<$). Next, when determining the other hypothesis, remember that H_0 and H_1 are complementary.

4. Distribution (Graphically): The "extract information" step includes a determination of the test statistic formula. Graph the distribution that accompanies that test statistic formula. Make sure that the shape of the graph matches the shape of the distribution. Label the horizontal axis with the letter associated with that distribution. Add the number of degrees of freedom, if applicable. Locate the tail(s). Remember that the tail(s) are described by H_1.

Critical Value Method (8-steps)

5. Critical Value(s): Using the appropriate table and the graph of the distribution from the "distribution (graphically)" step, find the critical value(s).

6. Test Statistic: The formula for the test statistic should already be included in this step from the "extract information" step. That step should also contain all of the values necessary to complete the calculation except for the value of the population parameters. The "null hypothesis, H_0" step is the working assumption for the hypothesis test and contains an equal sign so that the assumed value of the population parameters in H_0 may be used to find the value of test statistic. Find the value of the test statistic.

Critical Value Method (8-steps)

7. Statistical Conclusion: Compare the value of the test statistic to the critical value(s) and critical region graphed in the "distribution (graphically)" step. If the test statistic is in the critical region, reject H_0. If the test statistic is not in the critical region, fail to reject H_0. There are only two possible conclusions: "Fail to Reject H_0" or "Reject H_0". Any variation from these two possible conclusions is wrong.

8. Final Words: Consult the "Final Words" flowchart to determine the exact words necessary to complete this step. Information from the "Original Claim" step and the "Statistical Conclusion" step is required to select the correct wording. Every word must be written exactly as described in the "Final Words" flowchart, AND the wordy, non-math phrasing of the original claim (from the problem) must be substituted for "... [original claim]" in the final words. Any variation from this prescribed response is wrong.

Orange Marbles (One Proportion, Critical Value)

John purchases a bag of marbles and observes and counts their colors. The bag contains 142 marbles of which 11 are orange. Use the critical value method and a 7% significance level to test the claim that the percentage of orange marbles is at most 11%.

1. Extract Information:

2. Original Claim:	3. H_0:
	H_1:

Orange Marbles (One Proportion, Critical Value)

4. Distribution (Graphically):	6. Test Statistic:

	7. Statistical Conclusion:
5. Critical Value(s):	8. Final Words:

---

p-Value Method (8-steps)

1. Extract Information: Read. Read again. Read every single word including the small ones. Determine the population parameter being tested. Extract numerical information and assumptions from the problem. Assign statistics letters to the numbers from the problem. Determine the formula for the test statistic. Transfer the formula for the test statistic to the "test statistic" step. Do not calculate the value of the test statistic until reaching that step.

2. Original Claim: Using population parameters, translate the claim that is being tested into a mathematical sentence (better known as an equation or inequality). No words or sample statistics are expected in this step.

p-Value Method (8-steps)

3. Null Hypothesis, H_0, and Alternative Hypothesis, H_1: Transfer the original claim to either H_0 or H_1. The original claim—exactly as stated in the "original claim" step—must appear in either H_0 or H_1. Remember which mathematical sentences fit with H_0 (eg. $=$, $\leq$, $\geq$) and H_1 (eg. $\neq$, $>$, $<$). Next, when determining the other hypothesis, remember that H_0 and H_1 are complementary.

4. Test Statistic: The formula for the test statistic should already be included in this step from the "extract information" step. That step should also contain all of the values necessary to complete the calculation except for the value of the population parameters. The "null hypothesis, H_0" step is the working assumption for the hypothesis test and contains an equal sign so that the assumed value of the population parameters in H_0 may be used to find the value of test statistic. Find the value of the test statistic. Transfer the test statistic value to the edge of the appropriate tail on the "distribution (graphically)" step.

p-Value Method (8-steps)

5. Distribution (Graphically): The "extract information" step includes a determination of the test statistic formula. Graph the distribution that accompanies that test statistic formula. Make sure that the shape of the graph matches the shape of the distribution. Label the horizontal axis with the letter associated with that distribution. Add the number of degrees of freedom, if applicable. Locate the tail(s). Remember that the tail(s) are described by H_1.

6. *p*-value: Find the area of the tail bounded by the test statistic value. If the test is one-tailed, record the area of the tail as the *p*-value. If there are two-tails, remember that only one tail's boundary will be described by the test statistic value, and the *p*-value is twice the area of that tail. Also, it is possible that the boundary of the tail will be on the "wrong" side of the graph. This occurs when the *p*-value is extremely large (usually more than 50%).

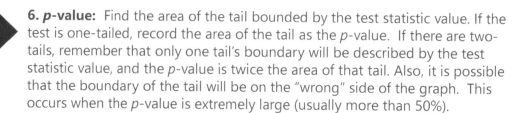

p-Value Method (8-steps)

7. Statistical Conclusion: Compare the *p*-value to the significance level, α. If $p \leq \alpha$, reject H_0. If $p > \alpha$, fail to reject H_0. There are only two possible conclusions: "Fail to Reject H_0" or "Reject H_0". Any variation from these two possible conclusions is wrong.

8. Final Words: Consult the "Final Words" flowchart to determine the exact words necessary to complete this step. Information from the "Original Claim" step and the "Statistical Conclusion" step is required to select the correct wording. Every word must be written exactly as described in the "Final Words" flowchart, AND the wordy, non-math phrasing of the original claim (from the problem) must be substituted for "... [original claim]" in the final words. Any variation from this prescribed response is wrong.

Orange Marbles (One Proportion, *p*-Value)

John purchases a bag of marbles and observes and counts their colors. The bag contains 142 marbles of which 11 are orange. Use the *p*-value method and a 7% significance level to test the claim that the percentage of orange marbles is at most 11%.

1. Extract Information:

2. Original Claim:	3. H_0:
	H_1:

Orange Marbles (One Proportion, *p*-Value)

4. Test Statistic:	6. *p*-Value:
5. Distribution (Graphically):	**7. Statistical Conclusion:**
	8. Final Words:

Section 16

8.3 Testing a Claim About a Mean
8.4 Testing a Claim About a Standard Deviation or Variance

Companion to *Elementary Statistics*, Thirteenth Edition and the Triola Stats Series, by Mario F. Triola.

Hypothesis Testing Methods

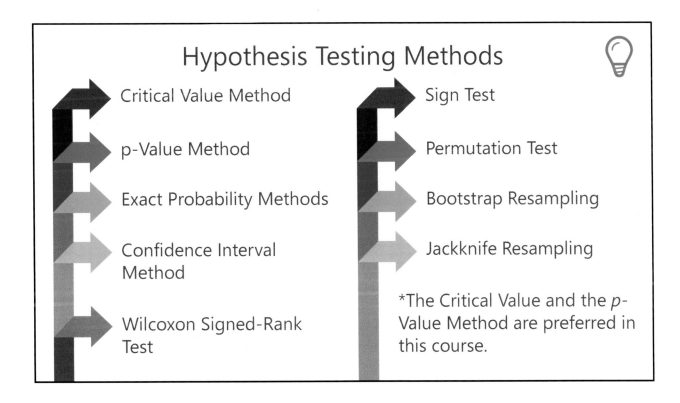

- Critical Value Method
- p-Value Method
- Exact Probability Methods
- Confidence Interval Method
- Wilcoxon Signed-Rank Test

- Sign Test
- Permutation Test
- Bootstrap Resampling
- Jackknife Resampling

*The Critical Value and the p-Value Method are preferred in this course.

Test Statistics for Testing One Population Parameter

Population Parameter	Conditions	Test Statistic	Distribution	Degrees of Freedom (df)	p-value
Mean, μ	• Simple Random Sample • Normally distributed population and/or $n>30$	$t = \dfrac{\bar{x} - \mu}{\dfrac{s}{\sqrt{n}}}$	Student t, Table A-3	n-1	Use technology or find high and low bounds for p from table.
	• Simple Random Sample • Normally distributed population and/or $n>30$ • σ is known	$z = \dfrac{\bar{x} - \mu}{\dfrac{\sigma}{\sqrt{n}}}$	Standard Normal z, Table A-2		Found on table.
Standard Deviation, σ	• Simple Random Sample • Normally distributed population	$\chi^2 = \dfrac{(n-1)s^2}{\sigma^2}$	Chi-square, χ^2 Table A-4	n-1	Use technology or find high and low bounds for p from table.
Proportion, p	• Simple Random Sample • Binomial Distribution Conditions • $n\hat{p} \geq 5$ and $n\hat{q} \geq 5$	$z = \dfrac{\hat{p} - p}{\sqrt{\dfrac{pq}{n}}}$	Standard Normal z, Table A-2		Found on table.

Final Words

It is very difficult to formulate the words of the final conclusion. ALWAYS consult this flowchart to determine the correct wording.

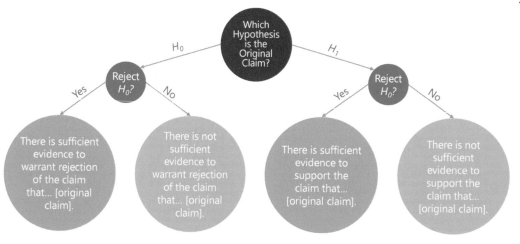

Heights of Women's Basketball Team (One Mean, Critical Value)

John wishes to study the heights of the women's basketball team. He completes a simple random sample of women's basketball team members. The results are listed below:

70, 71, 69.25, 68.5, 69, 70, 71, 70, 70, 69.5, 74, 75.5

John knows that women's heights are normally distributed. Use the critical value method and a 5% significance level to test the claim that women's basketball players have heights with a mean greater than 68.6 inches (population mean height of men).

1. Extract Information:	
2. Original Claim:	3. H_0: H_1:

142

Heights of Women's Basketball Team (One Mean, Critical Value)

4. Distribution (Graphically):

6. Test Statistic:

7. Statistical Conclusion:

8. Final Words:

5. Critical Value(s):

Human Body Temp (One Mean, *p*-Value)

John wishes to study the mean human body temperature. John organizes a simple random sample which allows him to measure the human body temperature of 45 people at school. His calculations show that his sample has a mean human body temperature of 98.40°F and a standard deviation of 0.62°F. Prior studies indicate that human body temperatures are normally distributed with a standard deviation of 0.50°F. Use the *p*-value method and a 2% significance level to test the claim that the mean human body temperature of the population is equal to 98.6°F as is commonly believed.

1. Extract Information:

2. Original Claim:

3. H_0:

H_1:

Human Body Temp (One Mean, *p*-Value)

4. Test Statistic:	6. *p*-Value:
5. Distribution (Graphically):	7. Statistical Conclusion:
	8. Final Words:

Highway Speeds (One Standard Deviation, Critical Value)

A highway engineer wishes to study highway speeds. Listed below is a simple random sample of speeds (mph) obtained at 4:48 PM on a weekday on the south 405 at Wilshire Blvd:

32, 31, 31, 27, 31, 24, 29, 28, 29, 39, 30, 37, 22, 25

Use the critical value method and a 5% significance level to test the claim that the standard deviation of the speeds is equal to 5.0 mph.

1. Extract Information:
2. Original Claim:

3. H_0:
H_1:

Highway Speeds (One Standard Deviation, Critical Value)

4. Distribution (Graphically):

5. Critical Value(s):

6. Test Statistic:

7. Statistical Conclusion:

8. Final Words:

Section 17

9.1 Two Proportions

9.2 Two Means: Independent Samples

Companion to *Elementary Statistics*, Thirteenth Edition and the Triola Stats Series, by Mario F. Triola.

Relationships Between Multiple Samples

INDEPENDENT — Two samples are independent if the sample values from one population are not related to or somehow naturally paired or matched with the sample values from the other population.

MATCHED PAIRS — Two samples are dependent (or consist of matched pairs) of the sample values are somehow matched, where the matching is based on some inherent relationship. Dependence does not require a direct cause/effect relationship

---

 # Confidence Intervals for Estimating Two Population Parameters

Population Parameter	Conditions	Confidence Interval	Distribution	Degrees of Freedom (df)
Mean, $\mu_1 - \mu_2$	• Simple Random Sample • Independent Samples • Normally distributed populations and/or $n_1 > 30$ and $n_2 > 30$	$P\left((\bar{x}_1 - \bar{x}_2) - E < (\mu_1 - \mu_2) < (\bar{x}_1 - \bar{x}_2) + E\right) = 1 - \alpha$ $E = t_{\alpha/2}\sqrt{\dfrac{s_1^2}{n_1} + \dfrac{s_2^2}{n_2}}$	Student t, Table A-3	Smaller of $n_1 - 1$ and $n_2 - 1$, or use technology
	• Simple Random Sample • Matched Pair Sample • Normally distributed difference-of-matched-pairs population and/or $n_d > 30$	$P(\bar{x}_d - E < \mu_d < \bar{x}_d + E) = 1 - \alpha$ $E = t_{\alpha/2}\dfrac{s_d}{\sqrt{n_d}}$	Student t, Table A-3	$n_d - 1$
Proportion, $p_1 - p_2$	• Simple Random Sample • Independent Samples • $n\hat{p}_1 \geq 5 \;\; n\hat{q}_1 \geq 5 \;\; n\hat{p}_2 \geq 5$ and $\; n\hat{q}_2 \geq 5$	$P\left((\hat{p}_1 - \hat{p}_2) - E < (p_1 - p_2) < (\hat{p}_1 - \hat{p}_2) + E)\right) = 1 - \alpha$ $E = z_{\alpha/2}\sqrt{\dfrac{\hat{p}_1\hat{q}_1}{n_1} + \dfrac{\hat{p}_2\hat{q}_2}{n_2}}$	Standard Normal z, Table A-2	

Test Statistics for Testing Two Population Parameters

Population Parameter	Conditions	Test Statistic	Distribution	Degrees of Freedom (df)	p-value
Mean, $\mu_1 - \mu_2$	• Simple Random Sample • Independent Samples • Normally distributed populations and/or $n_1 > 30$ and $n_2 > 30$	$t = \dfrac{(\bar{x}_1 - \bar{x}_2) - (\mu_1 - \mu_2)}{\sqrt{\dfrac{s_1^2}{n_1} + \dfrac{s_2^2}{n_2}}}$	Student t, Table A-3	Smaller of $n_1 - 1$ and $n_2 - 1$, or use technology	Use technology or find high and low bounds for p from table.
	• Simple Random Sample • Matched Pair Sample • Normally distributed difference-of-matched-pairs population and/or $n_d > 30$	$\mu_d = \mu_1 - \mu_2$ $t = \dfrac{\bar{x}_d - \mu_d}{\dfrac{s_d}{\sqrt{n_d}}}$ $x_d = x_1 - x_2$	Student t, Table A-3	$n_d - 1$	Use technology or find high and low bounds for p from table.
Standard Deviation, $\sigma_1 - \sigma_2$	• Simple Random Sample • Independent Samples • Normally distributed populations	$s_1^2 > s_2^2$ $F = \dfrac{s_1^2}{s_2^2}$	F, Table A-5 or F Table	$n_1 - 1$ Numerator & $n_2 - 1$ Denominator	Use technology or find high and low bounds for p from table.
Proportion, $p_1 - p_2$	• Simple Random Sample • Independent Samples • $n\hat{p}_1 \geq 5$, $n\hat{q}_1 \geq 5$, $n\hat{p}_2 \geq 5$, and $n\hat{q}_2 \geq 5$	$\bar{p} = \dfrac{x_1 + x_2}{n_1 + n_2}$ $z = \dfrac{(\hat{p}_1 - \hat{p}_2) - (p_1 - p_2)}{\sqrt{\dfrac{\bar{p}\bar{q}}{n_1} + \dfrac{\bar{p}\bar{q}}{n_2}}}$ $\bar{q} = 1 - \bar{p}$	Standard Normal z, Table A-2		Found on table.

Graveyard Shift (Two Proportion, Critical Value)

Among 343 women surveyed, 15 worked the graveyard shift. Among 294 men surveyed, 27 worked the graveyard shift. The samples are independent and were gathered using simple random sampling. Use the critical value method and a 1% significance level to test the claim that the proportion of women working the graveyard shift is less than the proportion of men working the graveyard shift.

1. Extract Information:

2. Original Claim:

3. H_0:

   H_1:

Graveyard Shift (Two Proportion, Critical Value)

4. Distribution (Graphically):

6. Test Statistic:

7. Statistical Conclusion:

8. Final Words:

5. Critical Value(s):

Dieters' Net Weight Change
(Two Means, Critical Value)

Based on a simple random sample of 52 juice-fast dieters, juice-fast dieters mean net weight change after three months is -21 pounds with a standard deviation of 12.4 pounds. Based on a simple random sample of 61 paleo dieters, paleo dieters mean net weight change after three months is -25 pounds with a standard deviation of 16.7 pounds. Use the critical value method and a 2% significance level to test the claim that juice-fast dieters and paleo dieters have the same mean net weight loss after three months.

1. Extract Information:

2. Original Claim:

3. H_0:

H_1:

Dieters' Net Weight Change
(Two Means, Critical Value)

4. Distribution (Graphically):	6. Test Statistic:
	7. Statistical Conclusion:
	8. Final Words:
5. Critical Value(s):	

Weights of Athletes (Two Means, *p*-Value)

Phil wishes to compare the weights of professional athletes to the weights of non-professional athletes. Phil completes a simple random sample of professional athletes and records his results in pounds (125, 147, 240, 186, 156, 205, 248, 152, 199, 207, 176). Phil also completes a simple random sample of non-professional athletes and records his results in pounds (151, 161, 139, 128, 149, 160, 201, 173). The samples are independent and come from normally distributed populations. Use the *p*-value method and a 2% significance level to test the claim that the mean weights of professional and non-professional athletes are the same.

1. Extract Information:	
2. Original Claim:	3. H_0:
	H_1:

Weights of Athletes (Two Means, p-Value)

4. Test Statistic:	6. p-Value:
5. Distribution (Graphically):	7. Statistical Conclusion:
	8. Final Words:

Section 18

9.3 Two Dependent Samples (Matched Pairs)
9.4 Two Variances or Standard Deviations

Companion to *Elementary Statistics*, Thirteenth Edition and the Triola Stats Series, by Mario F. Triola.

Confidence Intervals for Estimating Two Population Parameters

Population Parameter	Conditions	Confidence Interval	Distribution	Degrees of Freedom (df)
Mean, $\mu_1 - \mu_2$	• Simple Random Sample • Independent Samples • Normally distributed populations and/or $n_1 > 30$ and $n_2 > 30$	$P\big((\bar{x}_1 - \bar{x}_2) - E < (\mu_1 - \mu_2) < (\bar{x}_1 - \bar{x}_2) + E\big) = 1 - \alpha$ $E = t_{\alpha/2}\sqrt{\dfrac{s_1^2}{n_1} + \dfrac{s_2^2}{n_2}}$	Student t, Table A-3	Smaller of n_1-1 and n_2-1, or use technology
	• Simple Random Sample • Matched Pair Sample • Normally distributed difference-of-matched-pairs population and/or $n_d > 30$	$P(\bar{x}_d - E < \mu_d < \bar{x}_d + E) = 1 - \alpha$ $E = t_{\alpha/2}\dfrac{s_d}{\sqrt{n_d}}$	Student t, Table A-3	n_d-1
Proportion, $p_1 - p_2$	• Simple Random Sample • Independent Samples • $n\hat{p}_1 \geq 5$ $n\hat{q}_1 \geq 5$ $n\hat{p}_2 \geq 5$ and $n\hat{q}_2 \geq 5$	$P\big((\hat{p}_1 - \hat{p}_2) - E < (p_1 - p_2) < (\hat{p}_1 - \hat{p}_2) + E)\big) = 1 - \alpha$ $E = z_{\alpha/2}\sqrt{\dfrac{\hat{p}_1\hat{q}_1}{n_1} + \dfrac{\hat{p}_2\hat{q}_2}{n_2}}$	Standard Normal z, Table A-2	

Test Statistics for Testing Two Population Parameters

Population Parameter	Conditions	Test Statistic	Distribution	Degrees of Freedom (df)	p-value
Mean, $\mu_1 - \mu_2$	• Simple Random Sample • Independent Samples • Normally distributed populations and/or $n_1 > 30$ and $n_2 > 30$	$t = \dfrac{(\bar{x}_1 - \bar{x}_2) - (\mu_1 - \mu_2)}{\sqrt{\dfrac{s_1^2}{n_1} + \dfrac{s_2^2}{n_2}}}$	Student t, Table A-3	Smaller of n_1-1 and n_2-1, or use technology	Use technology or find high and low bounds for p from table.
	• Simple Random Sample • Matched Pair Sample • Normally distributed difference-of-matched-pairs population and/or $n_d > 30$	$\mu_d = \mu_1 - \mu_2$ $\quad t = \dfrac{\bar{x}_d - \mu_d}{\dfrac{s_d}{\sqrt{n_d}}}$ $x_d = x_1 - x_2$	Student t, Table A-3	n_d-1	Use technology or find high and low bounds for p from table.
Standard Deviation, $\sigma_1 - \sigma_2$	• Simple Random Sample • Independent Samples • Normally distributed populations	$s_1^2 > s_2^2 \qquad F = \dfrac{s_1^2}{s_2^2}$	F, Table A-5 or F Table	n_1-1 Numerator & n_2-1 Denominator	Use technology or find high and low bounds for p from table.
Proportion, $p_1 - p_2$	• Simple Random Sample • Independent Samples • $n\hat{p}_1 \geq 5$, $n\hat{q}_1 \geq 5$, $n\hat{p}_2 \geq 5$, and $n\hat{q}_2 \geq 5$	$\bar{p} = \dfrac{x_1 + x_2}{n_1 + n_2}$ $\quad z = \dfrac{(\hat{p}_1 - \hat{p}_2) - (p_1 - p_2)}{\sqrt{\dfrac{\overline{pq}}{n_1} + \dfrac{\overline{pq}}{n_2}}}$ $\bar{q} = 1 - \bar{p}$	Standard Normal z, Table A-2		Found on table.

F Distribution

The F distribution is a continuous probability distribution designed to compare variances, standard deviations, or other statistics from non-normal populations.

The F distribution is not symmetric.

The exact shape of the F distribution depends on the two different degrees of freedom.

Values of the F distribution cannot be negative.

Use Table A-5 or F Table to find critical values for the F distribution.

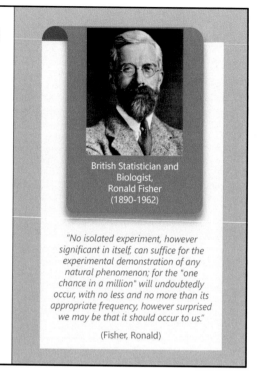

British Statistician and Biologist, Ronald Fisher (1890-1962)

"No isolated experiment, however significant in itself, can suffice for the experimental demonstration of any natural phenomenon; for the "one chance in a million" will undoubtedly occur, with no less and no more than its appropriate frequency, however surprised we may be that it should occur to us."

(Fisher, Ronald)

F Distribution (Graphically)

As numerator and denominator degrees of freedom increase, the *F* distribution becomes more symmetrical and closer to a normal distribution.

F Distribution at a significance level of 0.05 for 4/5, 40/5, 8/17, 24/25, and 60/120 degrees of freedom.

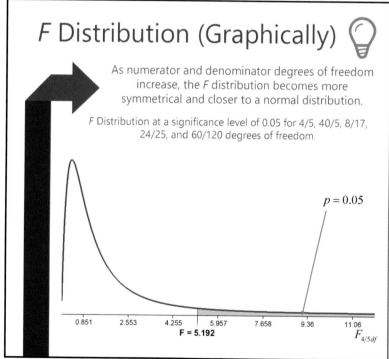

$p = 0.05$

| 0.851 | 2.553 | 4.255 | 5.957 | 7.658 | 9.36 | 11.06 |

F = 5.192

$F_{4/5df}$

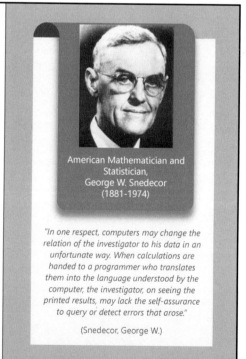

American Mathematician and Statistician, George W. Snedecor (1881-1974)

"In one respect, computers may change the relation of the investigator to his data in an unfortunate way. When calculations are handed to a programmer who translates them into the language understood by the computer, the investigator, on seeing the printed results, may lack the self-assurance to query or detect errors that arose."

(Snedecor, George W.)

Efficiency Expert (Matched Pairs, *p*-Value)

An efficiency expert is hired to improve productivity at a company. She administers an efficiency to test a simple random sample of the employees, implements a productivity training course, and administers the efficiency test again one month later to the same employees tested originally. The efficiency test results are below. Test score differences are known to come from a normally distributed population. Use the *p*-value method and a 8% significance level to test the claim that employee efficiency improved after the productivity training course.

1. Extract Information:

Employee #	#1	#2	#3	#4	#5	#6	#7	#8	#9	#10	#11	#12	#13	#14	#15
Before	21	25	45	28	23	27	22	28	39	35	34	40	27	20	33
After	32	25	36	47	37	30	40	39	28	48	28	41	27	33	28

2. Original Claim:

3. H_0:

   H_1:

Efficiency Expert (Matched Pairs, *p*-Value)

4. Test Statistic:

6. *p*-Value:

5. Distribution (Graphically):

7. Statistical Conclusion:

8. Final Words:

US Supreme Court (Two Standard Deviations, Critical Value)

There have been 16 US Supreme Court Chief Justices who have had the following tenures (in years):

18, 17, 15, 7, 4, 11, 8, 10, 21, 14, 8, 28, 34, 4, 0, 5

There have been 93 US Supreme Court Associate Justices who have had a mean tenure of 16.1720 years with a standard deviation of 9.871593 years. Use the critical value method and a 5% significance level to test the claim that the tenures of US Supreme Court Chief Justices have the same variation as the tenures of US Supreme Court Associate Justices.

1. Extract Information:

2. Original Claim:	3. H_0:
	H_1:

US Supreme Court (Two Standard Deviations, Critical Value)

4. Distribution (Graphically):	6. Test Statistic:
	7. Statistical Conclusion:
5. Critical Value(s):	8. Final Words:

Weights of Athletes
(Two Standard Deviations, *p*-Value)

Based on a simple random sample of 52 juice-fast dieters, juice-fast dieters mean net weight change after three months is -21 pounds with a standard deviation of 12.4 pounds. Based on a simple random sample of 61 paleo dieters, paleo dieters mean net weight change after three months is -25 pounds with a standard deviation of 16.7 pounds. Use the *p*-value method and a 3% significance level to test the claim that the weight of paleo dieters varies more than the weight of juice-fast dieters after three months.

1. Extract Information:

2. Original Claim:

3. H_0:

H_1:

Weights of Athletes
(Two Standard Deviations, *p*-Value)

4. Test Statistic:

6. *p*-Value:

5. Distribution (Graphically):

7. Statistical Conclusion:

8. Final Words:

Section 19

2.4 Scatterplots, Correlation, and Regression

10.1 Correlation

Companion to *Elementary Statistics*, Thirteenth Edition and the Triola Stats Series, by Mario F. Triola.

Characteristics of Data

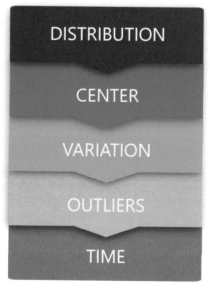

DISTRIBUTION — The nature or shape of the spread of data over the range of values (such as bell-shaped, uniform, or skewed).

CENTER — A representative value that indicates where the middle of the data set is located.

VARIATION — A measure of the amount that the data values vary.

OUTLIERS — Sample values that lie very far away from the vast majority of other sample values.

TIME — Changing characteristics of the data over time.

SCIENCE

Science is the intellectual and practical activity encompassing the systematic study of the structure and behavior of the physical and natural world through observation and experiment.

Power of Hypothesis Testing

A carefully formulated experiment may be performed to gather randomly-collected, unbiased data.

Unbiased observations based on a carefully formulated topic may be randomly-collected.

Hypothesis testing is designed to challenge the current scientific paradigm using this random, unbiased data. Remember that sometimes the results are, "there is sufficient evidence to support the claim." The power of the hypothesis test often changes society's understanding of the structure and behavior of the physical and natural world.

Correlation

CORRELATION — A correlation exists between two variables when the values of one variable are somehow associated with the values of the other variable.

LINEAR CORRELATION — A linear correlation exists between two variables when there is a correlation and the plotted points of paired data result in a pattern that can be approximated by a straight line.

SCATTERPLOT — A scatterplot (or scatter diagram) is a plot of *(x,y)* quantitative data with a horizontal *x*-axis and a vertical *y*-axis.

Linear Correlation Coefficient and Coefficient of Determination

The linear correlation coefficient (or Pearson product moment correlation coefficient), *r*, measures the strength of the linear correlation between the paired quantitative *x* and *y* values in a sample.

$$r = \frac{n\left(\sum xy\right) - \left(\sum x\right)\left(\sum y\right)}{\sqrt{n\left(\sum x^2\right) - \left(\sum x\right)^2}\sqrt{n\left(\sum y^2\right) - \left(\sum y\right)^2}}$$

Linear Correlation Coefficient, *r*

$$r^2$$

Coefficient of Determination (Explained Variation) which is the proportion of the variation in *y* that is explained by the linear relationship between *x* and *y*.

There are many different formulas for calculating the linear correlation coefficient, *r*. Each formula yields the same value of *r*. This is the least difficult formula for calculating *r* without the aid of technology.

Linear Correlation Coefficient, *r*

The linear correlation coefficient (or Pearson product moment correlation coefficient), *r*, measures the strength of the linear correlation between the paired quantitative *x* and *y* values in a sample.

The value of the linear correlation coefficient is always between -1 and 1, inclusive.

If all values of either variable are converted to a different scale, the value of *r* does not change.

The value of *r* is not affected by the choice of *x* and *y*. Interchange all *x*-values and *y*-values and the value of *r* will not change.

The value of the linear correlation coefficient is very sensitive (small changes to *(x,y)* result is large changes to *r*) to outliers.

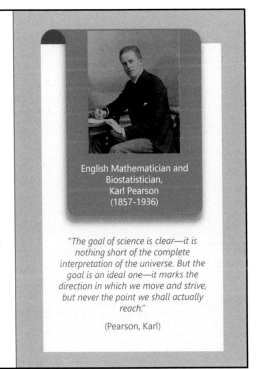

English Mathematician and Biostatistician, Karl Pearson (1857-1936)

"The goal of science is clear—it is nothing short of the complete interpretation of the universe. But the goal is an ideal one—it marks the direction in which we move and strive, but never the point we shall actually reach."

(Pearson, Karl)

Population Parameters & Sample Statistics

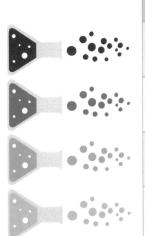

	Population Parameter	Sample Statistic
Mean	μ	$\overline{x}$
Standard Deviation	σ	s
Proportion	p	$\hat{p}$
Correlation Coefficient	ρ	r

Linear Correlation Coefficient, *r* (Scatterplots)

When *r* is close to zero, the data does not appear linear.

When *r* is positive, the slope of the linearity is positive.

When *r* is negative, the slope of the linearity is negative.

Scatterplots of paired data with *r* values of
r=-0.0650, *r*=0.1791, *r*=-0.8319, and *r*=0.9743.

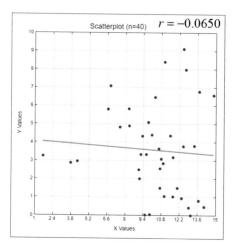

Common Errors Involving Correlation

Causation: It is wrong to conclude that correlation implies causality.

Averages: Averages suppress individual variation and may inflate the correlation coefficient.

Linearity: There may be some relationship between x and y even when there is no linear correlation.

 # Linear Correlation Test Statistic

Population Parameter	Conditions	Hypothesis	Test Statistic	Distribution	Degrees of Freedom (*df*)	*p*-value
Linear Correlation Coefficient, ρ	• Simple Random Sample of paired *(x,y)* data • Scatterplot is approximately a straight-line pattern • Carefully consider outliers • Bivariate Normal Distribution	Claim: $\rho \neq 0$ H_0: When $\rho = 0$, there is no linear correlation. H_1: When $\rho \neq 0$, there is not no linear correlation.	$t = \dfrac{r}{\sqrt{\dfrac{1-r^2}{n-2}}}$	Student *t*, Table A-3	*n*-2	Use technology or find high and low bounds for *p* from table.
			If |*r*|>critical value from Table A-6, reject H_0, and conclude, "There is sufficient evidence to support the claim that of linear correlation." If |*r*|≤critical value from Table A-6, fail to reject H_0, and conclude, "There is not sufficient evidence to support the claim that of linear correlation."	*r*, Table A-6	*n*	Use technology or find high and low bounds for *p* from table.

Unemployment (Linear Correlation, Critical Value)

Joe wishes to study the relationship between the Federal Reserve Board index of industrial production (FRBIP) and the unemployment rate (UR). The unemployment rate is the natural response variable. Use the critical value method and a 5% significance level to test the claim of linear correlation.

1. Extract Information:	**FRBIP, *x***	113	123	127	138	130	146	151	
	UR, *y*	3.1	1.9	1.7	1.6	3.2	2.7	2.6	

2. Original Claim:	3. H_0: H_1:

Unemployment (Linear Correlation, Critical Value)

4. Distribution (Graphically):

5. Critical Value(s):

6. Test Statistic:

7. Statistical Conclusion:

8. Final Words:

Heights of Children (Linear Correlation, *p*-Value)

Jane wishes to study the relationship between the mean heights in centimeters (H) of a group of 161 children in Kalama, an Egyptian village and the groups age in months (AGE). The height is the natural response variable. Use the *p*-value method and a 1% significance level to test the claim of linear correlation.

1. Extract Information:

AGE, x	18	19	21	22	24	25	27	28	
H, y	76.1	77.0	78.2	78.8	79.9	81.1	81.8	82.8	

2. Original Claim:

3. H_0:

H_1:

162

Heights of Children (Linear Correlation, *p*-Value)

4. Test Statistic:	6. *p*-Value:
5. Distribution (Graphically):	7. Statistical Conclusion:
	8. Final Words:

Section 20

10.2 Regression
10.3 Prediction Intervals and Variation

Companion to *Elementary Statistics*, Thirteenth Edition and the Triola Stats Series, by Mario F. Triola.

 # Linear Correlation Test Statistic

Population Parameter	Conditions	Hypothesis	Test Statistic	Distribution	Degrees of Freedom (df)	p-value
Linear Correlation Coefficient, ρ	• Simple Random Sample of paired (x,y) data • Scatterplot is approximately a straight-line pattern • Carefully consider outliers • Bivariate Normal Distribution	Claim: $\rho \neq 0$ H_0: When $\rho = 0$, there is no linear correlation. H_1: When $\rho \neq 0$, there is not no linear correlation.	$$t = \frac{r}{\sqrt{\dfrac{1-r^2}{n-2}}}$$	Student t, Table A-3	$n-2$	Use technology or find high and low bounds for p from table.
			If $|r| >$ critical value from Table A-6, reject H_0, and conclude, "There is sufficient evidence to support the claim that of linear correlation." If $|r| \leq$ critical value from Table A-6, fail to reject H_0, and conclude, "There is not sufficient evidence to support the claim that of linear correlation."	r, Table A-6	n	Use technology or find high and low bounds for p from table.

Regression Analysis

REGRESSION LINE

Given a collection of paired sample data, the regression line (or line-of-best-fit or least-squares line) is the straight line that "best" fits the scatterplot of the data.

LINEAR CORRELATION

The regression equation algebraically describes the regression line. The regression equation expresses a relationship between x (called the explanatory variable or predictor variable or independent variable) and $\hat{y}$ (called the response variable or dependent variable).

PREDICTION INTERVAL

A prediction interval is a range of values used to estimate a variable (like y in a regression equation). They are similar to confidence intervals, except confidence intervals estimate population parameters.

Power of Regression Analysis

Regression analysis generates a relationship between a predictor variable and a response variable allowing scientists to predict the response variable when supplying a predictor variable.

Regression analysis is designed to predict the outcome of a unknown scenario based on similar scenarios and outcomes that have occurred in the past. In this way, regression analysis is almost like predicting the future or divining the unknown. The power of regression analysis lies in its ability to know the structure and behavior of the physical and natural world without prior experience of the exact situation being considered.

Regression Population Parameters & Sample Statistics

	Population Parameter	Sample Statistic
Predictor variable not present in the data	x_0	x_0
Predictor variable present in the data	x	x
Response variable in the population	y	
Response variable predicted by the sample regression equation		$\hat{y}$
y-intercept	β_0	b_0
Slope	β_1	b_1
Regression Equation	$y = \beta_0 + \beta_1 x$	$\hat{y} = b_0 + b_1 x$

Regression Line

$$\hat{y} = b_0 + b_1 x$$
Regression Line

$$b_1 = \frac{n\left(\sum xy\right) - \left(\sum x\right)\left(\sum y\right)}{n\left(\sum x^2\right) - \left(\sum x\right)^2}$$
Slope, b_1

$$b_0 = \frac{\left(\sum y\right)\left(\sum x^2\right) - \left(\sum x\right)\left(\sum xy\right)}{n\left(\sum x^2\right) - \left(\sum x\right)^2}$$
y-intercept, b_0

There are many different formulas for calculating and the y-intercept, b_0. the slope, b_1. Each formula yields the same value of b_0 and b_1. These are the least difficult formulas for calculating b_0 and b_1 without the aid of technology.

Regression Line

Use the regression line for predictions ONLY IF the graph of the regression line on the scatterplot confirms that the regression line fits the points reasonably well.

Use the regression line for predictions ONLY IF the linear correlation coefficient, r, indicates that there is a linear correlation between the two variables.

Use the regression line for predictions ONLY IF the data do not go much beyond the scope of the available sample data.

If the sample data does not support the claim of linearity, the best predicted value of the dependent variable is the dependent variable's sample mean, $\bar{y}$.

 # Standard Error of Estimate, s_e

The standard error of estimate, s_e, is a measure of variation of the differences between the observed, sample values, y, and the predicted values, $\hat{y}$.

$$s_e = \sqrt{\frac{\left(\sum y^2\right) - b_0\left(\sum y\right) - b_1\left(\sum xy\right)}{n-2}}$$ Standard Error of Estimate, s_e

There are many different formulas for calculating the standard error of estimate, s_e. Each formula yields the same value of s_e. This is the least difficult formula for calculating s_e without the aid of technology.

 # Prediction Interval for Response Variable, y

Population Parameter	Conditions	Confidence Interval	Distribution	Degrees of Freedom (df)
Response Variable, y	• Simple Random Sample of paired (x,y) data • Scatterplot is approximately a straight-line pattern • Carefully consider outliers • Bivariate Normal Distribution	$P\left(\hat{y} - E < y < \hat{y} + E\right) = 1 - \alpha$ $E = \left(t_{\alpha/2}\right)\left(s_e\right)\sqrt{1 + \frac{1}{n} + \frac{n\left(x_0 - \frac{\sum x}{n}\right)^2}{n\left(\sum x^2\right) - \left(\sum x\right)^2}}$	Student t, Table A-3	$n-2$

Regression & Prediction Interval Procedure

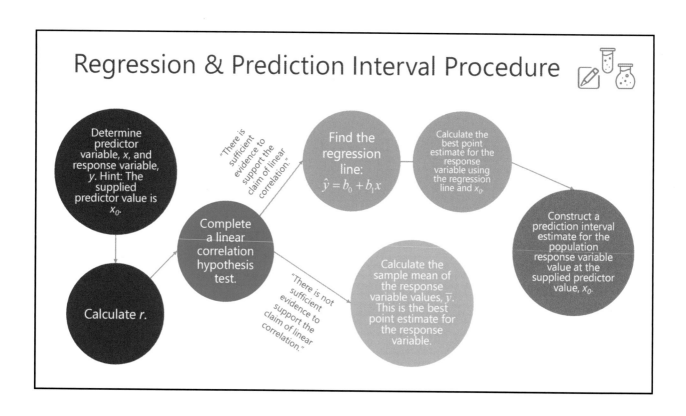

Breast Cancer Mortality and Temperature (Regression and Prediction Interval)

Bob wishes to study the relationship between mean annual temperature (Temp) and the mortality rate (SMI) for a type of breast cancer in women at a 5% significance level and collects paired sample data. Determine predictor variable, x, and response variable, y.

Calculate r.

SMI	100	96	95	89	89	79	82	72	65	68	53	
Temp	50	49	48	47	45	46	44	43	42	40	34	

Breast Cancer Mortality and Temperature (Regression and Prediction Interval)

Is there sufficient evidence support the claim of linear correlation? Why? (Hint: Complete a linear correlation hypothesis test.)

Find the regression line.

Breast Cancer Mortality and Temperature (Regression and Prediction Interval)

Calculate the best point estimate for the mortality rate (SMI) for a type of breast cancer in women at mean annual temperature (Temp) of 38.

Construct a prediction interval estimate for SMI at a Temp of 38.

Section 21

11.1 Goodness-of-Fit
11.2 Contingency Tables

Companion to *Elementary Statistics*, Thirteenth Edition and the Triola Stats Series, by Mario F. Triola.

Frequency Distribution Hypothesis Testing

GOODNESS-OF-FIT
A goodness-of-fit test is used to test the hypothesis that an observed frequency distribution fits (or conforms to) some claimed frequency distribution.

CONTIGENCY TABLE
A contingency table (or a two-way frequency table) is a table frequency counts of categorical data corresponding to two different variables.

TEST OF INDEPENDENCE
A test of independence tests the null hypothesis that in a contingency table, the row and column variables are independent.

TEST OF HOMOGENEITY
In a test of homogeneity, we test the claim that different populations have the same proportions of some characteristics.

Goodness-of-Fit Notation

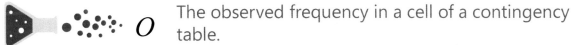
O The observed frequency in a cell of a contingency table.

E The expected frequency in a cell, found by assuming that the row and column variables are independent

k The number of different categories or cells.

n The total number of trials (or total of observed sample values).

p The probability that a sample value falls within a particular category.

Contingency Table Notation

O The observed frequency in a cell of a contingency table.

E The expected frequency in a cell, found by assuming that the row and column variables are independent

r The number of rows in a contingency table (not including labels).

c The number of columns in a contingency table (not including labels).

Independence Versus Homogeneity

In a typical test of independence, sample subjects are randomly selected from one population and values of two different variables are observed. Two variables' relative frequencies are compared to one another within one populations.

In a test of homogeneity, subjects are randomly selected from the different populations separately. One variable's relative frequencies are compared across multiple populations.

Test Statistics Frequency Distributions

Population Parameter	Conditions	Hypotheses	Expected Frequencies, E	Test Statistic and Distribution	Degrees of Freedom (df)	p-value
Goodness-of-Fit	• Simple Random Sample • Data are frequency counts for each of the different categories. • E is at least 5 each category. (O has no requirements.)	H_0: Frequency counts agree with claimed distribution. H_1: Frequency counts do not agree with claimed distribution.	$E = np$ Unequal expected frequencies. (Calculate E values for each category.) $E = \dfrac{n}{k}$ Equal expected frequencies. (One E value for all cells.)	$\chi^2 = \sum \dfrac{(O-E)^2}{E}$ Chi-square, χ^2 Table A-4 (always right-tailed)	$k-1$	Use technology or find high and low bounds for p from table.
Independence	• Simple Random Samples • Data are frequency counts in a two-way table. • E is at least 5 each category. (O has no requirements.)	H_0: Row and column variables are independent. H_1: Row and column variables are dependent.	$E_{i,j} = \dfrac{R_i C_j}{N}$ E_{ij} is the expected frequency for the cell in the ith row and the jth column. R_i is the total number of counts in the ith row. C_j is the total number of counts in the jth column. N is the total number of counts in the table.		$(r-1)(c-1)$	
Homogeneity		H_0: The populations are homogeneous. H_1: The populations are heterogeneous.				

Cents on Checks (Goodness-of-Fit, p-Value)

A simple random sample of checks were categorized based on the number of cents on the written check and recorded below. Use the p-value method and a 5% significance level to test the claim that 50% of the check population falls into the 0¢-24¢ category, 20% of the check population falls into the 25¢-49¢ category, 16% of the check population falls into the 50¢-74¢ category, and 14% of the check population falls into the 75¢-99¢ category.

1. Extract Information:

Cents Category	0¢-24¢		25¢-49¢		50¢-74¢		75¢-99¢			
Frequency	58		37		28		17			

2. Original Claim:

3. H_0:

   H_1:

Cents on Checks (Goodness-of-Fit, p-Value)

4. Test Statistic:

6. p-Value:

5. Distribution (Graphically):

7. Statistical Conclusion:

8. Final Words:

Dental Restoration (Independence, Critical Value)

A simple random sample of dental procedures was categorized based on the type of restoration and the occurrence of an adverse reaction. Use the critical value method and a 10% significance level to test the claim that adverse health reactions are independent of dental restoration types.

1. Extract Information:

Dental Procedures	Amalgam Restoration		Composite Restoration		
Adverse Reaction	135		145		
No Reaction	100		120		

2. Original Claim:

3. H_0:

   H_1:

Dental Restoration (Independence, Critical Value)

4. Distribution (Graphically):

5. Critical Value(s):

6. Test Statistic:

7. Statistical Conclusion:

8. Final Words:

Working Mothers (Homogeneity, *p*-Value)

A simple random sample of school children was categorized based on the level of school and the children's preference for a mother working outside the home. Use the *p*-value method and a 0.5% significance level to test the claim that the populations of elementary school children, middle school children, and high school children exhibit homogeneous preferences for working mothers.

1. Extract Information:

Working Mothers	Elementary School Children		Middle School Children		High School Children	
Prefer	37		48		89	
No Preference	63		52		11	

2. Original Claim:

3. H_0:

H_1:

Working Mothers (Homogeneity, *p*-Value)

4. Test Statistic:

6. *p*-Value:

5. Distribution (Graphically):

7. Statistical Conclusion:

8. Final Words:

Section 22

12.1 One-Way ANOVA

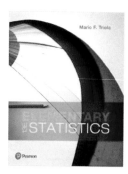

Companion to *Elementary Statistics*, Thirteenth Edition and the Triola Stats Series, by Mario F. Triola.

Statistics Roadmap

CHAP 1	Data and Sampling
CHAP 2-3	Descriptive Statistics and Graphing (what actually did happen)
CHAP 4	Probability
CHAP 5-6	Probability Distributions of Discrete and Continuous Variables (what probably will happen)
CHAP 7-12	Inferential Statistics ("Comparison" of what probably will happen to what actually did happen generating "conclusions" about the data.

Discrete Data Hypothesis Testing

PROPORTIONS

ONE PROPORTION	Chapter 8; one population; compare one proportion to a value
TWO PROPORTIONS	Chapter 9; two populations; compare one proportion to another proportion
MORE THAN TWO PROPORTIONS	Chapter 11; one population; compare cells of frequency distributions (Goodness-of-Fit)
	Chapter 11; one population; compare cells of contingency tables (Independence)
	Chapter 11; two or more populations; compare rows or columns of contingency tables (Homogeneity)

Continuous Data Hypothesis Testing

MEANS

ONE MEAN	Chapter 8; one population; compare one mean to a value
TWO MEANS	Chapter 9; two populations; compare one mean to another mean
MORE THAN TWO MEANS	Chapter 12; more than two populations; test the equality of more than two means (One-Way ANOVA)

Continuous Data Hypothesis Testing

VARIANCE (STANDARD DEVIATION)

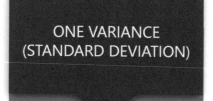

ONE VARIANCE (STANDARD DEVIATION) — Chapter 8; one population; compare one variance (standard deviation) to a value

TWO VARIANCES (STANDARD DEVIATIONS) — Chapter 9; two populations; compare one variance (standard deviation) to another variance (standard deviation)

Test Statistics Frequency Distributions

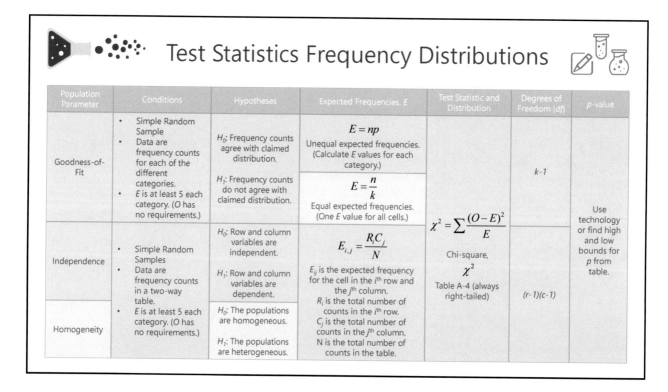

Population Parameter	Conditions	Hypotheses	Expected Frequencies, E	Test Statistic and Distribution	Degrees of Freedom (df)	p-value
Goodness-of-Fit	• Simple Random Sample • Data are frequency counts for each of the different categories. • E is at least 5 each category. (O has no requirements.)	H_0: Frequency counts agree with claimed distribution. H_1: Frequency counts do not agree with claimed distribution.	$E = np$ Unequal expected frequencies. (Calculate E values for each category.) $E = \dfrac{n}{k}$ Equal expected frequencies. (One E value for all cells.)	$\chi^2 = \sum \dfrac{(O-E)^2}{E}$ Chi-square, χ^2 Table A-4 (always right-tailed)	k-1	Use technology or find high and low bounds for p from table.
Independence	• Simple Random Samples • Data are frequency counts in a two-way table. • E is at least 5 each category. (O has no requirements.)	H_0: Row and column variables are independent. H_1: Row and column variables are dependent.	$E_{i,j} = \dfrac{R_i C_j}{N}$ E_{ij} is the expected frequency for the cell in the ith row and the jth column. R_i is the total number of counts in the ith row. C_j is the total number of counts in the jth column. N is the total number of counts in the table.		$(r$-$1)(c$-$1)$	
Homogeneity		H_0: The populations are homogeneous. H_1: The populations are heterogeneous.				

178

Cents on Checks (Goodness-of-Fit, Critical Value)

A simple random sample of checks were categorized based on the number of cents on the written check and recorded below. Use the critical value method and a 1% significance level to test the claim that the frequencies of the cents categories of checks fit the uniform distribution.

1. Extract Information:

Cents Category	0¢-24¢	25¢-49¢	50¢-74¢	75¢-99¢		
Frequency	58	37	28	17		

2. Original Claim:

3. H_0:

   H_1:

Cents on Checks (Goodness-of-Fit, Critical Value)

4. Distribution (Graphically):

5. Critical Value(s):

6. Test Statistic:

7. Statistical Conclusion:

8. Final Words:

ONE-WAY ANOVA

One-way analysis of variance (ANOVA) is a method of testing the equality of more than two population means by analyzing sample variances.

One-way analysis of variance is used with data categorized with one factor (or treatment), which is a characteristic that allows us to distinguish the different populations from one another.

One-Way ANOVA

ANOVA calculations are tedious and difficult and are usually completed exclusively with technology; however, the one-way ANOVA calculations used to test the claim of equality of more than two population means where equal sample sizes are taken from each population are possible without the aid of technology.

When we conclude that there is sufficient evidence to reject the claim of equal population means, we cannot conclude from ANOVA that any particular mean is different from the others.

Test Statistics One-Way ANOVA

Population Parameter	Conditions	Hypotheses	Calculations	Test Statistic	Distribution	Degrees of Freedom (df)	p-value
One-Way ANOVA	• Populations have approximately normal distributions. • Populations have the same variance. • Simple random samples of continuous data. • Independent Samples • The different samples are from populations that are categorized in only one way.	H_0: $\mu_1=\mu_2=\mu_3= \ldots$ H_1: At least one is different.	$ns_{\bar{x}}^2$ = variance between samples. $s_{\bar{x}}^2$ = variance of the sample means. s_p^2 = mean of the sample variances.	$F = \dfrac{ns_{\bar{x}}^2}{s_p^2}$	F, Table A-5 or F Table (always right-tailed)	$k\text{-}1$ Numerator & $k(n\text{-}1)$ Denominator	Use technology or find high and low bounds for p from table.

Tree Weights (One-Way ANOVA, *p*-Value)

Simple random samples of tree weights (kg) after treatments with nothing, fertilizer, irrigation, or both are listed below. The samples were independent and taken from normally distributed populations with the same variance. Use the *p*-value method and a 5% significance level to test the claim that the treatment samples come from populations with the same mean weight.

1. Extract Information:

Tree #	#1	#2	#3	#4	#5			
Nothing	0.24	1.69	1.23	0.99	1.80			
Fertilizer	0.92	0.07	0.56	1.74	1.13			
Irrigation	0.96	1.43	1.26	1.57	0.72			
Both	2.07	2.63	1.59	1.49	1.95			

2. Original Claim:

3. H_0:

H_1:

Tree Weights (One-Way ANOVA, *p*-Value)

4. Test Statistic:	6. *p*-Value:
5. Distribution (Graphically):	7. Statistical Conclusion:
	8. Final Words:

Highway Speeds (One-Way ANOVA, Critical Value)

Simple random samples of speeds (mph) obtained at 4:36 PM on a Monday, Tuesday, Wednesday, Thursday, and Friday on the south 405 at Wilshire Blvd are listed below. The samples were independent and taken from normally distributed populations with the same variance. Use the critical value method and a 5% significance level to test the claim that the daily samples come from populations with the same mean speeds.

1. Extract Information:

Car #	#1	#2	#3	#4	#5	#6	#7	#8	#9	#10	#11			
Monday	20	20	33	45	39	27	5	28	35	17	22			
Tuesday	27	33	25	36	40	30	12	6	7	24	41			
Wednesday	23	34	27	9	19	22	41	28	0	23	33			
Thursday	37	32	47	0	13	40	14	3	41	21	16			
Friday	11	27	39	28	48	21	28	15	33	18	5			

| 2. Original Claim: | 3. H_0: |
| | H_1: |

Highway Speeds (One-Way ANOVA, Critical Value)

4. Distribution (Graphically):

6. Test Statistic:

7. Statistical Conclusion:

8. Final Words:

5. Critical Value(s):

NEGATIVE z Scores

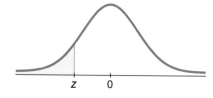

z   0

TABLE A-2 Standard Normal (z) Distribution: Cumulative Area from the LEFT

z	.00	.01	.02	.03	.04	.05	.06	.07	.08	.09
−3.50 and lower	.0001									
−3.4	.0003	.0003	.0003	.0003	.0003	.0003	.0003	.0003	.0003	.0002
−3.3	.0005	.0005	.0005	.0004	.0004	.0004	.0004	.0004	.0004	.0003
−3.2	.0007	.0007	.0006	.0006	.0006	.0006	.0006	.0005	.0005	.0005
−3.1	.0010	.0009	.0009	.0009	.0008	.0008	.0008	.0008	.0007	.0007
−3.0	.0013	.0013	.0013	.0012	.0012	.0011	.0011	.0011	.0010	.0010
−2.9	.0019	.0018	.0018	.0017	.0016	.0016	.0015	.0015	.0014	.0014
−2.8	.0026	.0025	.0024	.0023	.0023	.0022	.0021	.0021	.0020	.0019
−2.7	.0035	.0034	.0033	.0032	.0031	.0030	.0029	.0028	.0027	.0026
−2.6	.0047	.0045	.0044	.0043	.0041	.0040	.0039	.0038	.0037	.0036
−2.5	.0062	.0060	.0059	.0057	.0055	.0054	.0052	.0051 *	.0049	.0048
−2.4	.0082	.0080	.0078	.0075	.0073	.0071	.0069	.0068	.0066	.0064
−2.3	.0107	.0104	.0102	.0099	.0096	.0094	.0091	.0089	.0087	.0084
−2.2	.0139	.0136	.0132	.0129	.0125	.0122	.0119	.0116	.0113	.0110
−2.1	.0179	.0174	.0170	.0166	.0162	.0158	.0154	.0150	.0146	.0143
−2.0	.0228	.0222	.0217	.0212	.0207	.0202	.0197	.0192	.0188	.0183
−1.9	.0287	.0281	.0274	.0268	.0262	.0256	.0250	.0244	.0239	.0233
−1.8	.0359	.0351	.0344	.0336	.0329	.0322	.0314	.0307	.0301	.0294
−1.7	.0446	.0436	.0427	.0418	.0409	.0401	.0392	.0384	.0375	.0367
−1.6	.0548	.0537	.0526	.0516	.0505 *	.0495	.0485	.0475	.0465	.0455
−1.5	.0668	.0655	.0643	.0630	.0618	.0606	.0594	.0582	.0571	.0559
−1.4	.0808	.0793	.0778	.0764	.0749	.0735	.0721	.0708	.0694	.0681
−1.3	.0968	.0951	.0934	.0918	.0901	.0885	.0869	.0853	.0838	.0823
−1.2	.1151	.1131	.1112	.1093	.1075	.1056	.1038	.1020	.1003	.0985
−1.1	.1357	.1335	.1314	.1292	.1271	.1251	.1230	.1210	.1190	.1170
−1.0	.1587	.1562	.1539	.1515	.1492	.1469	.1446	.1423	.1401	.1379
−0.9	.1841	.1814	.1788	.1762	.1736	.1711	.1685	.1660	.1635	.1611
−0.8	.2119	.2090	.2061	.2033	.2005	.1977	.1949	.1922	.1894	.1867
−0.7	.2420	.2389	.2358	.2327	.2296	.2266	.2236	.2206	.2177	.2148
−0.6	.2743	.2709	.2676	.2643	.2611	.2578	.2546	.2514	.2483	.2451
−0.5	.3085	.3050	.3015	.2981	.2946	.2912	.2877	.2843	.2810	.2776
−0.4	.3446	.3409	.3372	.3336	.3300	.3264	.3228	.3192	.3156	.3121
−0.3	.3821	.3783	.3745	.3707	.3669	.3632	.3594	.3557	.3520	.3483
−0.2	.4207	.4168	.4129	.4090	.4052	.4013	.3974	.3936	.3897	.3859
−0.1	.4602	.4562	.4522	.4483	.4443	.4404	.4364	.4325	.4286	.4247
−0.0	.5000	.4960	.4920	.4880	.4840	.4801	.4761	.4721	.4681	.4641

NOTE: For values of z below −3.49, use 0.0001 for the area.
*Use these common values that result from interpolation:

(*continued*)

z Score	Area
−1.645	0.0500
−2.575	0.0050

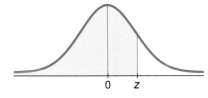

POSITIVE z Scores

TABLE A-2 *(continued)* Cumulative Area from the LEFT

z	.00	.01	.02	.03	.04	.05	.06	.07	.08	.09
0.0	.5000	.5040	.5080	.5120	.5160	.5199	.5239	.5279	.5319	.5359
0.1	.5398	.5438	.5478	.5517	.5557	.5596	.5636	.5675	.5714	.5753
0.2	.5793	.5832	.5871	.5910	.5948	.5987	.6026	.6064	.6103	.6141
0.3	.6179	.6217	.6255	.6293	.6331	.6368	.6406	.6443	.6480	.6517
0.4	.6554	.6591	.6628	.6664	.6700	.6736	.6772	.6808	.6844	.6879
0.5	.6915	.6950	.6985	.7019	.7054	.7088	.7123	.7157	.7190	.7224
0.6	.7257	.7291	.7324	.7357	.7389	.7422	.7454	.7486	.7517	.7549
0.7	.7580	.7611	.7642	.7673	.7704	.7734	.7764	.7794	.7823	.7852
0.8	.7881	.7910	.7939	.7967	.7995	.8023	.8051	.8078	.8106	.8133
0.9	.8159	.8186	.8212	.8238	.8264	.8289	.8315	.8340	.8365	.8389
1.0	.8413	.8438	.8461	.8485	.8508	.8531	.8554	.8577	.8599	.8621
1.1	.8643	.8665	.8686	.8708	.8729	.8749	.8770	.8790	.8810	.8830
1.2	.8849	.8869	.8888	.8907	.8925	.8944	.8962	.8980	.8997	.9015
1.3	.9032	.9049	.9066	.9082	.9099	.9115	.9131	.9147	.9162	.9177
1.4	.9192	.9207	.9222	.9236	.9251	.9265	.9279	.9292	.9306	.9319
1.5	.9332	.9345	.9357	.9370	.9382	.9394	.9406	.9418	.9429	.9441
1.6	.9452	.9463	.9474	.9484	.9495 *	.9505	.9515	.9525	.9535	.9545
1.7	.9554	.9564	.9573	.9582	.9591	.9599	.9608	.9616	.9625	.9633
1.8	.9641	.9649	.9656	.9664	.9671	.9678	.9686	.9693	.9699	.9706
1.9	.9713	.9719	.9726	.9732	.9738	.9744	.9750	.9756	.9761	.9767
2.0	.9772	.9778	.9783	.9788	.9793	.9798	.9803	.9808	.9812	.9817
2.1	.9821	.9826	.9830	.9834	.9838	.9842	.9846	.9850	.9854	.9857
2.2	.9861	.9864	.9868	.9871	.9875	.9878	.9881	.9884	.9887	.9890
2.3	.9893	.9896	.9898	.9901	.9904	.9906	.9909	.9911	.9913	.9916
2.4	.9918	.9920	.9922	.9925	.9927	.9929	.9931	.9932	.9934	.9936
2.5	.9938	.9940	.9941	.9943	.9945	.9946	.9948	.9949 *	.9951	.9952
2.6	.9953	.9955	.9956	.9957	.9959	.9960	.9961	.9962	.9963	.9964
2.7	.9965	.9966	.9967	.9968	.9969	.9970	.9971	.9972	.9973	.9974
2.8	.9974	.9975	.9976	.9977	.9977	.9978	.9979	.9979	.9980	.9981
2.9	.9981	.9982	.9982	.9983	.9984	.9984	.9985	.9985	.9986	.9986
3.0	.9987	.9987	.9987	.9988	.9988	.9989	.9989	.9989	.9990	.9990
3.1	.9990	.9991	.9991	.9991	.9992	.9992	.9992	.9992	.9993	.9993
3.2	.9993	.9993	.9994	.9994	.9994	.9994	.9994	.9995	.9995	.9995
3.3	.9995	.9995	.9995	.9996	.9996	.9996	.9996	.9996	.9996	.9997
3.4	.9997	.9997	.9997	.9997	.9997	.9997	.9997	.9997	.9997	.9998
3.50 and up	.9999									

NOTE: For values of z above 3.49, use 0.9999 for the area.
*Use these common values that result from interpolation:

z score	Area
1.645	0.9500
2.575	0.9950

Common Critical Values

Confidence Level	Critical Value
0.90	1.645
0.95	1.96
0.99	2.575

TABLE A-3 *t* Distribution: Critical *t* Values

Degrees of Freedom	Area in One Tail				
	0.005	0.01	0.025	0.05	0.10
	Area in Two Tails				
	0.01	0.02	0.05	0.10	0.20
1	63.657	31.821	12.706	6.314	3.078
2	9.925	6.965	4.303	2.920	1.886
3	5.841	4.541	3.182	2.353	1.638
4	4.604	3.747	2.776	2.132	1.533
5	4.032	3.365	2.571	2.015	1.476
6	3.707	3.143	2.447	1.943	1.440
7	3.499	2.998	2.365	1.895	1.415
8	3.355	2.896	2.306	1.860	1.397
9	3.250	2.821	2.262	1.833	1.383
10	3.169	2.764	2.228	1.812	1.372
11	3.106	2.718	2.201	1.796	1.363
12	3.055	2.681	2.179	1.782	1.356
13	3.012	2.650	2.160	1.771	1.350
14	2.977	2.624	2.145	1.761	1.345
15	2.947	2.602	2.131	1.753	1.341
16	2.921	2.583	2.120	1.746	1.337
17	2.898	2.567	2.110	1.740	1.333
18	2.878	2.552	2.101	1.734	1.330
19	2.861	2.539	2.093	1.729	1.328
20	2.845	2.528	2.086	1.725	1.325
21	2.831	2.518	2.080	1.721	1.323
22	2.819	2.508	2.074	1.717	1.321
23	2.807	2.500	2.069	1.714	1.319
24	2.797	2.492	2.064	1.711	1.318
25	2.787	2.485	2.060	1.708	1.316
26	2.779	2.479	2.056	1.706	1.315
27	2.771	2.473	2.052	1.703	1.314
28	2.763	2.467	2.048	1.701	1.313
29	2.756	2.462	2.045	1.699	1.311
30	2.750	2.457	2.042	1.697	1.310
31	2.744	2.453	2.040	1.696	1.309
32	2.738	2.449	2.037	1.694	1.309
33	2.733	2.445	2.035	1.692	1.308
34	2.728	2.441	2.032	1.691	1.307
35	2.724	2.438	2.030	1.690	1.306
36	2.719	2.434	2.028	1.688	1.306
37	2.715	2.431	2.026	1.687	1.305
38	2.712	2.429	2.024	1.686	1.304
39	2.708	2.426	2.023	1.685	1.304
40	2.704	2.423	2.021	1.684	1.303
45	2.690	2.412	2.014	1.679	1.301
50	2.678	2.403	2.009	1.676	1.299
60	2.660	2.390	2.000	1.671	1.296
70	2.648	2.381	1.994	1.667	1.294
80	2.639	2.374	1.990	1.664	1.292
90	2.632	2.368	1.987	1.662	1.291
100	2.626	2.364	1.984	1.660	1.290
200	2.601	2.345	1.972	1.653	1.286
300	2.592	2.339	1.968	1.650	1.284
400	2.588	2.336	1.966	1.649	1.284
500	2.586	2.334	1.965	1.648	1.283
1000	2.581	2.330	1.962	1.646	1.282
2000	2.578	2.328	1.961	1.646	1.282
Large	2.576	2.326	1.960	1.645	1.282

TABLE A-4 Chi-Square (χ^2) Distribution

Degrees of Freedom	Area to the *Right* of the Critical Value									
	0.995	0.99	0.975	0.95	0.90	0.10	0.05	0.025	0.01	0.005
1	—	—	0.001	0.004	0.016	2.706	3.841	5.024	6.635	7.879
2	0.010	0.020	0.051	0.103	0.211	4.605	5.991	7.378	9.210	10.597
3	0.072	0.115	0.216	0.352	0.584	6.251	7.815	9.348	11.345	12.838
4	0.207	0.297	0.484	0.711	1.064	7.779	9.488	11.143	13.277	14.860
5	0.412	0.554	0.831	1.145	1.610	9.236	11.071	12.833	15.086	16.750
6	0.676	0.872	1.237	1.635	2.204	10.645	12.592	14.449	16.812	18.548
7	0.989	1.239	1.690	2.167	2.833	12.017	14.067	16.013	18.475	20.278
8	1.344	1.646	2.180	2.733	3.490	13.362	15.507	17.535	20.090	21.955
9	1.735	2.088	2.700	3.325	4.168	14.684	16.919	19.023	21.666	23.589
10	2.156	2.558	3.247	3.940	4.865	15.987	18.307	20.483	23.209	25.188
11	2.603	3.053	3.816	4.575	5.578	17.275	19.675	21.920	24.725	26.757
12	3.074	3.571	4.404	5.226	6.304	18.549	21.026	23.337	26.217	28.299
13	3.565	4.107	5.009	5.892	7.042	19.812	22.362	24.736	27.688	29.819
14	4.075	4.660	5.629	6.571	7.790	21.064	23.685	26.119	29.141	31.319
15	4.601	5.229	6.262	7.261	8.547	22.307	24.996	27.488	30.578	32.801
16	5.142	5.812	6.908	7.962	9.312	23.542	26.296	28.845	32.000	34.267
17	5.697	6.408	7.564	8.672	10.085	24.769	27.587	30.191	33.409	35.718
18	6.265	7.015	8.231	9.390	10.865	25.989	28.869	31.526	34.805	37.156
19	6.844	7.633	8.907	10.117	11.651	27.204	30.144	32.852	36.191	38.582
20	7.434	8.260	9.591	10.851	12.443	28.412	31.410	34.170	37.566	39.997
21	8.034	8.897	10.283	11.591	13.240	29.615	32.671	35.479	38.932	41.401
22	8.643	9.542	10.982	12.338	14.042	30.813	33.924	36.781	40.289	42.796
23	9.260	10.196	11.689	13.091	14.848	32.007	35.172	38.076	41.638	44.181
24	9.886	10.856	12.401	13.848	15.659	33.196	36.415	39.364	42.980	45.559
25	10.520	11.524	13.120	14.611	16.473	34.382	37.652	40.646	44.314	46.928
26	11.160	12.198	13.844	15.379	17.292	35.563	38.885	41.923	45.642	48.290
27	11.808	12.879	14.573	16.151	18.114	36.741	40.113	43.194	46.963	49.645
28	12.461	13.565	15.308	16.928	18.939	37.916	41.337	44.461	48.278	50.993
29	13.121	14.257	16.047	17.708	19.768	39.087	42.557	45.722	49.588	52.336
30	13.787	14.954	16.791	18.493	20.599	40.256	43.773	46.979	50.892	53.672
40	20.707	22.164	24.433	26.509	29.051	51.805	55.758	59.342	63.691	66.766
50	27.991	29.707	32.357	34.764	37.689	63.167	67.505	71.420	76.154	79.490
60	35.534	37.485	40.482	43.188	46.459	74.397	79.082	83.298	88.379	91.952
70	43.275	45.442	48.758	51.739	55.329	85.527	90.531	95.023	100.425	104.215
80	51.172	53.540	57.153	60.391	64.278	96.578	101.879	106.629	112.329	116.321
90	59.196	61.754	65.647	69.126	73.291	107.565	113.145	118.136	124.116	128.299
100	67.328	70.065	74.222	77.929	82.358	118.498	124.342	129.561	135.807	140.169

Source: From Donald B. Owen, *Handbook of Statistical Tables.*

Degrees of Freedom

$n - 1$	Confidence Interval or Hypothesis Test for a standard deviation or variance
$k - 1$	Goodness-of-fit test with k different categories
$(r - 1)(c - 1)$	Contingency table test with r rows and c columns
$k - 1$	Kruskal-Wallis test with k different samples

Formulas and Tables by Mario F. Triola
Copyright 2018 Pearson Education, Inc.

Ch. 3: Descriptive Statistics

$\bar{x} = \dfrac{\Sigma x}{n}$ Mean

$\bar{x} = \dfrac{\Sigma (f \cdot x)}{\Sigma f}$ Mean (frequency table)

$s = \sqrt{\dfrac{\Sigma (x - \bar{x})^2}{n - 1}}$ Standard deviation

$s = \sqrt{\dfrac{n(\Sigma x^2) - (\Sigma x)^2}{n(n - 1)}}$ Standard deviation (shortcut)

$s = \sqrt{\dfrac{n[\Sigma (f \cdot x^2)] - [\Sigma (f \cdot x)]^2}{n(n - 1)}}$ Standard deviation (frequency table)

$\text{variance} = s^2$

Ch. 4: Probability

$P(A \text{ or } B) = P(A) + P(B)$ if A, B are mutually exclusive

$P(A \text{ or } B) = P(A) + P(B) - P(A \text{ and } B)$
   if A, B are not mutually exclusive

$P(A \text{ and } B) = P(A) \cdot P(B)$ if A, B are independent

$P(A \text{ and } B) = P(A) \cdot P(B|A)$ if A, B are dependent

$P(\bar{A}) = 1 - P(A)$ Rule of complements

$_nP_r = \dfrac{n!}{(n - r)!}$ Permutations (no elements alike)

$\dfrac{n!}{n_1! \, n_2! \, \ldots \, n_k!}$ Permutations (n_1 alike, ...)

$_nC_r = \dfrac{n!}{(n - r)! \, r!}$ Combinations

Ch. 5: Probability Distributions

$\mu = \Sigma [x \cdot P(x)]$ Mean (prob. dist.)

$\sigma = \sqrt{\Sigma [x^2 \cdot P(x)] - \mu^2}$ Standard deviation (prob. dist.)

$P(x) = \dfrac{n!}{(n - x)! \, x!} \cdot p^x \cdot q^{n-x}$ Binomial probability

$\mu = n \cdot p$ Mean (binomial)

$\sigma^2 = n \cdot p \cdot q$ Variance (binomial)

$\sigma = \sqrt{n \cdot p \cdot q}$ Standard deviation (binomial)

$P(x) = \dfrac{\mu^x \cdot e^{-\mu}}{x!}$ Poisson distribution where $e = 2.71828$

Ch. 6: Normal Distribution

$z = \dfrac{x - \mu}{\sigma}$ or $\dfrac{x - \bar{x}}{s}$ Standard score

$\mu_{\bar{x}} = \mu$ Central limit theorem

$\sigma_{\bar{x}} = \dfrac{\sigma}{\sqrt{n}}$ Central limit theorem (Standard error)

Ch. 7: Confidence Intervals (one population)

$\hat{p} - E < p < \hat{p} + E$ Proportion

where $E = z_{\alpha/2} \sqrt{\dfrac{\hat{p}\hat{q}}{n}}$

$\bar{x} - E < \mu < \bar{x} + E$ Mean

where $E = t_{\alpha/2} \dfrac{s}{\sqrt{n}}$ (σ unknown)

or $E = z_{\alpha/2} \dfrac{\sigma}{\sqrt{n}}$ (σ known)

$\dfrac{(n - 1)s^2}{\chi_R^2} < \sigma^2 < \dfrac{(n - 1)s^2}{\chi_L^2}$ Variance

Ch. 7: Sample Size Determination

$n = \dfrac{[z_{\alpha/2}]^2 0.25}{E^2}$ Proportion

$n = \dfrac{[z_{\alpha/2}]^2 \hat{p}\hat{q}}{E^2}$ Proportion ($\hat{p}$ and $\hat{q}$ are known)

$n = \left[\dfrac{z_{\alpha/2}\sigma}{E} \right]^2$ Mean

Ch. 8: Test Statistics (one population)

$z = \dfrac{\hat{p} - p}{\sqrt{\dfrac{pq}{n}}}$ Proportion—one population

$t = \dfrac{\bar{x} - \mu}{\dfrac{s}{\sqrt{n}}}$ Mean—one population (σ unknown)

$z = \dfrac{\bar{x} - \mu}{\dfrac{\sigma}{\sqrt{n}}}$ Mean—one population (σ known)

$\chi^2 = \dfrac{(n - 1)s^2}{\sigma^2}$ Standard deviation or variance—one population

Formulas and Tables by Mario F. Triola
Copyright 2018 Pearson Education, Inc.

Ch. 9: Confidence Intervals (two populations)

$$(\hat{p}_1 - \hat{p}_2) - E < (p_1 - p_2) < (\hat{p}_1 - \hat{p}_2) + E$$

where $E = z_{\alpha/2}\sqrt{\dfrac{\hat{p}_1\hat{q}_1}{n_1} + \dfrac{\hat{p}_2\hat{q}_2}{n_2}}$

$(\bar{x}_1 - \bar{x}_2) - E < (\mu_1 - \mu_2) < (\bar{x}_1 - \bar{x}_2) + E$ (Indep.)

where $E = t_{\alpha/2}\sqrt{\dfrac{s_1^2}{n_1} + \dfrac{s_2^2}{n_2}}$ (df = smaller of $n_1 - 1, n_2 - 1$)

(σ_1 and σ_2 unknown and not assumed equal)

$$E = t_{\alpha/2}\sqrt{\dfrac{s_p^2}{n_1} + \dfrac{s_p^2}{n_2}} \quad (\text{df} = n_1 + n_2 - 2)$$

$$s_p^2 = \dfrac{(n_1 - 1)s_1^2 + (n_2 - 1)s_2^2}{(n_1 - 1) + (n_2 - 1)}$$

(σ_1 and σ_2 unknown but assumed equal)

$$E = z_{\alpha/2}\sqrt{\dfrac{\sigma_1^2}{n_1} + \dfrac{\sigma_2^2}{n_2}}$$

(σ_1, σ_2 known)

$\bar{d} - E < \mu_d < \bar{d} + E$ (Matched pairs)

where $E = t_{\alpha/2}\dfrac{s_d}{\sqrt{n}}$ (df = n − 1)

Ch. 9: Test Statistics (two populations)

$$z = \dfrac{(\hat{p}_1 - \hat{p}_2) - (p_1 - p_2)}{\sqrt{\dfrac{\bar{p}\,\bar{q}}{n_1} + \dfrac{\bar{p}\,\bar{q}}{n_2}}} \quad \begin{array}{l}\text{Two proportions} \\ \bar{p} = \dfrac{x_1 + x_2}{n_1 + n_2}\end{array}$$

$$t = \dfrac{(\bar{x}_1 - \bar{x}_2) - (\mu_1 - \mu_2)}{\sqrt{\dfrac{s_1^2}{n_1} + \dfrac{s_2^2}{n_2}}} \quad \begin{array}{l}\text{df = smaller of} \\ n_1 - 1, n_2 - 1\end{array}$$

Two means—independent; σ_1 and σ_2 unknown, and not assumed equal.

$$t = \dfrac{(\bar{x}_1 - \bar{x}_2) - (\mu_1 - \mu_2)}{\sqrt{\dfrac{s_p^2}{n_1} + \dfrac{s_p^2}{n_2}}} \quad (\text{df} = n_1 + n_2 - 2)$$

$$s_p^2 = \dfrac{(n_1 - 1)s_1^2 + (n_2 - 1)s_2^2}{n_1 + n_2 - 2}$$

Two means—independent; σ_1 and σ_2 unknown, but assumed equal.

$$z = \dfrac{(\bar{x}_1 - \bar{x}_2) - (\mu_1 - \mu_2)}{\sqrt{\dfrac{\sigma_1^2}{n_1} + \dfrac{\sigma_2^2}{n_2}}} \quad \begin{array}{l}\text{Two means—independent;} \\ \sigma_1, \sigma_2 \text{ known.}\end{array}$$

$$t = \dfrac{\bar{d} - \mu_d}{\dfrac{s_d}{\sqrt{n}}} \quad \text{Two means—matched pairs (df = n − 1)}$$

$$F = \dfrac{s_1^2}{s_2^2} \quad \begin{array}{l}\text{Standard deviation or variance—} \\ \text{two populations (where } s_1^2 \geq s_2^2)\end{array}$$

Ch. 10: Linear Correlation/Regression

Correlation $r = \dfrac{n\Sigma xy - (\Sigma x)(\Sigma y)}{\sqrt{n(\Sigma x^2) - (\Sigma x)^2}\sqrt{n(\Sigma y^2) - (\Sigma y)^2}}$

or $r = \dfrac{\Sigma(z_x z_y)}{n - 1}$ where z_x = z score for x, z_y = z score for y

---

Slope: $b_1 = \dfrac{n\Sigma xy - (\Sigma x)(\Sigma y)}{n(\Sigma x^2) - (\Sigma x)^2}$ or $b_1 = r\dfrac{s_y}{s_x}$

y-Intercept:

$b_0 = \bar{y} - b_1\bar{x}$ or $b_0 = \dfrac{(\Sigma y)(\Sigma x^2) - (\Sigma x)(\Sigma xy)}{n(\Sigma x^2) - (\Sigma x)^2}$

$\hat{y} = b_0 + b_1 x$ Estimated eq. of regression line

$r^2 = \dfrac{\text{explained variation}}{\text{total variation}}$

$s_e = \sqrt{\dfrac{\Sigma(y - \hat{y})^2}{n - 2}}$ or $\sqrt{\dfrac{\Sigma y^2 - b_0\Sigma y - b_1\Sigma xy}{n - 2}}$

$\hat{y} - E < y < \hat{y} + E$ Prediction interval

where $E = t_{\alpha/2}s_e\sqrt{1 + \dfrac{1}{n} + \dfrac{n(x_0 - \bar{x})^2}{n(\Sigma x^2) - (\Sigma x)^2}}$

Ch. 11: Goodness-of-Fit and Contingency Tables

$\chi^2 = \Sigma\dfrac{(O - E)^2}{E}$ Goodness-of-fit (df = k − 1)

$\chi^2 = \Sigma\dfrac{(O - E)^2}{E}$ Contingency table [df = (r − 1)(c − 1)]

where $E = \dfrac{(\text{row total})(\text{column total})}{(\text{grand total})}$

$\chi^2 = \dfrac{(|b - c| - 1)^2}{b + c}$ McNemar's test for matched pairs (df = 1)

Ch. 12: One-Way Analysis of Variance

Procedure for testing $H_0: \mu_1 = \mu_2 = \mu_3 = \ldots$

1. Use software or calculator to obtain results.
2. Identify the P-value.
3. Form conclusion:

   If P-value $\leq \alpha$, reject the null hypothesis of equal means.

   If P-value $> \alpha$, fail to reject the null hypothesis of equal means.

Ch. 12: Two-Way Analysis of Variance

Procedure:

1. Use software or a calculator to obtain results.
2. Test H_0: There is no interaction between the row factor and column factor.
3. Stop if H_0 from Step 2 is rejected.

   If H_0 from Step 2 is not rejected (so there does not appear to be an interaction effect), proceed with these two tests:
   Test for effects from the row factor.
   Test for effects from the column factor.

Ch. 13: Nonparametric Tests

$$z = \frac{(x + 0.5) - (n/2)}{\frac{\sqrt{n}}{2}} \quad \text{Sign test for } n > 25$$

$$z = \frac{T - n(n + 1)/4}{\sqrt{\frac{n(n + 1)(2n + 1)}{24}}} \quad \begin{array}{l}\text{Wilcoxon signed ranks}\\ \text{(matched pairs and } n > 30)\end{array}$$

$$z = \frac{R - \mu_R}{\sigma_R} = \frac{R - \frac{n_1(n_1 + n_2 + 1)}{2}}{\sqrt{\frac{n_1 n_2(n_1 + n_2 + 1)}{12}}} \quad \begin{array}{l}\text{Wilcoxon rank-sum}\\ \text{(two independent}\\ \text{samples)}\end{array}$$

$$H = \frac{12}{N(N + 1)}\left(\frac{R_1^2}{n_1} + \frac{R_2^2}{n_2} + \cdots + \frac{R_k^2}{n_k}\right) - 3(N + 1)$$

Kruskal-Wallis (chi-square df $= k - 1$)

$$r_s = 1 - \frac{6\Sigma d^2}{n(n^2 - 1)} \quad \text{Rank correlation}$$

$$\left(\text{critical values for } n > 30: \frac{\pm z}{\sqrt{n - 1}}\right)$$

$$z = \frac{G - \mu_G}{\sigma_G} = \frac{G - \left(\frac{2n_1 n_2}{n_1 + n_2} + 1\right)}{\sqrt{\frac{(2n_1 n_2)(2n_1 n_2 - n_1 - n_2)}{(n_1 + n_2)^2(n_1 + n_2 - 1)}}} \quad \begin{array}{l}\text{Runs test}\\ \text{for } n > 20\end{array}$$

Ch. 14: Control Charts

R chart: Plot sample ranges

UCL: $D_4\overline{R}$

Centerline: $\overline{R}$

LCL: $D_3\overline{R}$

$\overline{x}$ chart: Plot sample means

UCL: $\overline{\overline{x}} + A_2\overline{R}$

Centerline: $\overline{\overline{x}}$

LCL: $\overline{\overline{x}} - A_2\overline{R}$

p chart: Plot sample proportions

UCL: $\overline{p} + 3\sqrt{\frac{\overline{p}\,\overline{q}}{n}}$

Centerline: $\overline{p}$

LCL: $\overline{p} - 3\sqrt{\frac{\overline{p}\,\overline{q}}{n}}$

TABLE A-6 Critical Values of the Pearson Correlation Coefficient r

n	$\alpha = .05$	$\alpha = .01$
4	.950	.990
5	.878	.959
6	.811	.917
7	.754	.875
8	.707	.834
9	.666	.798
10	.632	.765
11	.602	.735
12	.576	.708
13	.553	.684
14	.532	.661
15	.514	.641
16	.497	.623
17	.482	.606
18	.468	.590
19	.456	.575
20	.444	.561
25	.396	.505
30	.361	.463
35	.335	.430
40	.312	.402
45	.294	.378
50	.279	.361
60	.254	.330
70	.236	.305
80	.220	.286
90	.207	.269
100	.196	.256

NOTE: To test $H_0: \rho = 0$ (no correlation) against $H_1: \rho \neq 0$ (correlation), reject H_0 if the absolute value of r is greater than or equal to the critical value in the table.

Control Chart Constants

Subgroup Size n	D_3	D_4	A_2
2	0.000	3.267	1.880
3	0.000	2.574	1.023
4	0.000	2.282	0.729
5	0.000	2.114	0.577
6	0.000	2.004	0.483
7	0.076	1.924	0.419

Inferences about μ: choosing between t and normal distributions	
t distribution: or	σ not known and normally distributed population σ not known and $n > 30$
Normal distribution: or	σ known and normally distributed population σ known and $n > 30$
Nonparametric method or bootstrapping: Population not normally distributed and $n \leq 30$	

Procedure for Hypothesis Tests

1. Identify the Claim
Identify the claim to be tested and express it in symbolic form.

2. Give Symbolic Form
Give the symbolic form that must be true when the original claim is false.

3. Identify Null and Alternative Hypothesis
Consider the two symbolic expressions obtained so far:
- **Alternative hypothesis H_1** is the one *NOT* containing equality, so H_1 uses the symbol $>$ or $<$ or $\neq$.
- **Null hypothesis H_0** is the symbolic expression that the parameter equals the fixed value being considered.

4. Select Significance Level
Select the **significance level α** based on the seriousness of a type I error. Make α small if the consequences of rejecting a true H_0 are severe.
- The values of 0.05 and 0.01 are very common.

5. Identify the Test Statistic
Identify the test statistic that is relevant to the test and determine its sampling distribution (such as normal, t, chi-square).

P-Value Method

6. Find Values
Find the value of the **test statistic** and the **P-value** (see Figure 8-3). Draw a graph and show the test statistic and P-value.

7. Make a Decision
- **Reject H_0** if P-value $\leq \alpha$.
- **Fail to reject H_0** if P-value $> \alpha$.

Critical Value Method

6. Find Values
Find the value of the **test statistic** and the **critical values**. Draw a graph showing the test statistic, critical value(s) and critical region.

7. Make a Decision
- **Reject H_0** if the test statistic is in the critical region.
- **Fail to reject H_0** if the test statistic is not in the critical region.

8. Restate Decision in Nontechnical Terms
Restate this previous decision in simple nontechnical terms, and address the original claim.

Finding *P*-Values

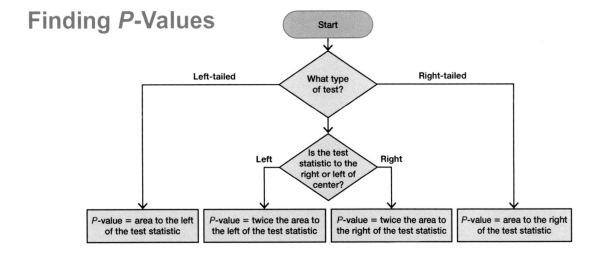

F Table for $\alpha = 0.025$

$F(df_1, df_2)$

Special Thanks to:
Ivo Dinov
UCLA Statistics, Neurology, LONI
http://www.socr.ucla.edu/Applets.dir/F_Table.html

$df_{denominator}$ \ $df_{numerator}$	1	2	3	4	5	6	7	8	9	10	12	15	20	24	30	40	60	120	∞
1	647.7890	799.5000	864.1630	899.5833	921.8479	937.1111	948.2169	956.6562	963.2846	968.6274	976.7079	984.8668	993.1028	997.2492	1001.414	1005.598	1009.800	1014.020	1018.258
2	38.5063	39.0000	39.1655	39.2484	39.2982	39.3315	39.3552	39.3730	39.3869	39.3980	39.4146	39.4313	39.4479	39.4562	39.4646	39.473	39.481	39.490	39.498
3	17.4434	16.0441	15.4392	15.1010	14.8848	14.7347	14.6244	14.5399	14.4731	14.4189	14.3366	14.2527	14.1674	14.1241	14.081	14.037	13.992	13.947	13.902
4	12.2179	10.6491	9.9792	9.6045	9.3645	9.1973	9.0741	8.9796	8.9047	8.8439	8.7512	8.6565	8.5599	8.5109	8.4613	8.4111	8.3604	8.3092	8.2573
5	10.0070	8.4336	7.7636	7.3879	7.1464	6.9777	6.8531	6.7572	6.6811	6.6192	6.5245	6.4277	6.3286	6.2780	6.2269	6.1750	6.1225	6.0693	6.0153
6	8.8131	7.2599	6.5988	6.2272	5.9876	5.8198	5.6955	5.5996	5.5234	5.4613	5.3662	5.2687	5.1684	5.1172	5.0652	5.0125	4.9589	4.9044	4.8491
7	8.0727	6.5415	5.8898	5.5226	5.2852	5.1186	4.9949	4.8993	4.8232	4.7611	4.6658	4.5678	4.4667	4.4150	4.3624	4.3089	4.2544	4.1989	4.1423
8	7.5709	6.0595	5.4160	5.0526	4.8173	4.6517	4.5286	4.4333	4.3572	4.2951	4.1997	4.1012	3.9995	3.9472	3.8940	3.8398	3.7844	3.7279	3.6702
9	7.2093	5.7147	5.0781	4.7181	4.4844	4.3197	4.1970	4.1020	4.0260	3.9639	3.8682	3.7694	3.6669	3.6142	3.5604	3.5055	3.4493	3.3918	3.3329
10	6.9367	5.4564	4.8256	4.4683	4.2361	4.0721	3.9498	3.8549	3.7790	3.7168	3.6209	3.5217	3.4185	3.3654	3.3110	3.2554	3.1984	3.1399	3.0798
11	6.7241	5.2559	4.6300	4.2751	4.0440	3.8807	3.7586	3.6638	3.5879	3.5257	3.4296	3.3299	3.2261	3.1725	3.1176	3.0613	3.0035	2.9441	2.8828
12	6.5538	5.0959	4.4742	4.1212	3.8911	3.7283	3.6065	3.5118	3.4358	3.3736	3.2773	3.1772	3.0728	3.0187	2.9633	2.9063	2.8478	2.7874	2.7249
13	6.4143	4.9653	4.3472	3.9959	3.7667	3.6043	3.4827	3.3880	3.3120	3.2497	3.1532	3.0527	2.9477	2.8932	2.8372	2.7797	2.7204	2.6590	2.5955
14	6.2979	4.8567	4.2417	3.8919	3.6634	3.5014	3.3799	3.2853	3.2093	3.1469	3.0502	2.9493	2.8437	2.7888	2.7324	2.6742	2.6142	2.5519	2.4872
15	6.1995	4.7650	4.1528	3.8043	3.5764	3.4147	3.2934	3.1987	3.1227	3.0602	2.9633	2.8621	2.7559	2.7006	2.6437	2.5850	2.5242	2.4611	2.3953
16	6.1151	4.6867	4.0768	3.7294	3.5021	3.3406	3.2194	3.1248	3.0488	2.9862	2.8890	2.7875	2.6808	2.6252	2.5678	2.5085	2.4471	2.3831	2.3163
17	6.0420	4.6189	4.0112	3.6648	3.4379	3.2767	3.1556	3.0610	2.9849	2.9222	2.8249	2.7230	2.6158	2.5598	2.5020	2.4422	2.3801	2.3153	2.2474
18	5.9781	4.5597	3.9539	3.6083	3.3820	3.2209	3.0999	3.0053	2.9291	2.8664	2.7689	2.6667	2.5590	2.5027	2.4445	2.3842	2.3214	2.2558	2.1869
19	5.9216	4.5075	3.9034	3.5587	3.3327	3.1718	3.0509	2.9563	2.8801	2.8172	2.7196	2.6171	2.5089	2.4523	2.3937	2.3329	2.2696	2.2032	2.1333
20	5.8715	4.4613	3.8587	3.5147	3.2891	3.1283	3.0074	2.9128	2.8365	2.7737	2.6758	2.5731	2.4645	2.4076	2.3486	2.2873	2.2234	2.1562	2.0853
21	5.8266	4.4199	3.8188	3.4754	3.2501	3.0895	2.9686	2.8740	2.7977	2.7348	2.6368	2.5338	2.4247	2.3675	2.3082	2.2465	2.1819	2.1141	2.0422
22	5.7863	4.3828	3.7829	3.4401	3.2151	3.0546	2.9338	2.8392	2.7628	2.6998	2.6017	2.4984	2.3890	2.3315	2.2718	2.2097	2.1446	2.0760	2.0032
23	5.7498	4.3492	3.7505	3.4083	3.1835	3.0232	2.9023	2.8077	2.7313	2.6682	2.5699	2.4665	2.3567	2.2989	2.2389	2.1763	2.1107	2.0415	1.9677
24	5.7166	4.3187	3.7211	3.3794	3.1548	2.9946	2.8738	2.7791	2.7027	2.6396	2.5411	2.4374	2.3273	2.2693	2.2090	2.1460	2.0799	2.0099	1.9353
25	5.6864	4.2909	3.6943	3.3530	3.1287	2.9685	2.8478	2.7531	2.6766	2.6135	2.5149	2.4110	2.3005	2.2422	2.1816	2.1183	2.0516	1.9811	1.9055
26	5.6586	4.2655	3.6697	3.3289	3.1048	2.9447	2.8240	2.7293	2.6528	2.5896	2.4908	2.3867	2.2759	2.2174	2.1565	2.0928	2.0257	1.9545	1.8781
27	5.6331	4.2421	3.6472	3.3067	3.0828	2.9228	2.8021	2.7074	2.6309	2.5676	2.4688	2.3644	2.2533	2.1946	2.1334	2.0693	2.0018	1.9299	1.8527
28	5.6096	4.2205	3.6264	3.2863	3.0626	2.9027	2.7820	2.6872	2.6106	2.5473	2.4484	2.3438	2.2324	2.1735	2.1121	2.0477	1.9797	1.9072	1.8291
29	5.5878	4.2006	3.6072	3.2674	3.0438	2.8840	2.7633	2.6686	2.5919	2.5286	2.4295	2.3248	2.2131	2.1540	2.0923	2.0276	1.9591	1.8861	1.8072
30	5.5675	4.1821	3.5894	3.2499	3.0265	2.8667	2.7460	2.6513	2.5746	2.5112	2.4120	2.3072	2.1952	2.1359	2.0739	2.0089	1.9400	1.8664	1.7867
40	5.4239	4.0510	3.4633	3.1261	2.9037	2.7444	2.6238	2.5289	2.4519	2.3882	2.2882	2.1819	2.0677	2.0069	1.9429	1.8752	1.8028	1.7242	1.6371
60	5.2856	3.9253	3.3425	3.0077	2.7863	2.6274	2.5068	2.4117	2.3344	2.2702	2.1692	2.0613	1.9445	1.8817	1.8152	1.7440	1.6668	1.5810	1.4821
120	5.1523	3.8046	3.2269	2.8943	2.6740	2.5154	2.3948	2.2994	2.2217	2.1570	2.0548	1.9450	1.8249	1.7597	1.6899	1.6141	1.5299	1.4327	1.3104
∞	5.0239	3.6889	3.1161	2.7858	2.5665	2.4082	2.2875	2.1918	2.1136	2.0483	1.9447	1.8326	1.7085	1.6402	1.5660	1.4835	1.3883	1.2684	1.0000

Special Thanks to:
Ivo Dinov
UCLA Statistics, Neurology, LONI
http://www.socr.ucla.edu/Applets.dir/F_Table.html

F Table for α = 0.05

$F(df_1, df_2)$

df$_{denominator}$ \ df$_{numerator}$	1	2	3	4	5	6	7	8	9	10	12	15	20	24	30	40	60	120	∞
1	161.4476	199.5000	215.7073	224.5832	230.1619	233.9860	236.7684	238.8827	240.5433	241.8817	243.9060	245.9499	248.0131	249.0518	250.0951	251.1432	252.1957	253.2529	254.3144
2	18.5128	19.0000	19.1643	19.2468	19.2964	19.3295	19.3532	19.3710	19.3848	19.3959	19.4125	19.4291	19.4458	19.4541	19.4624	19.4707	19.4791	19.4874	19.4957
3	10.1280	9.5521	9.2766	9.1172	9.0135	8.9406	8.8867	8.8452	8.8123	8.7855	8.7446	8.7029	8.6602	8.6385	8.6166	8.5944	8.5720	8.5494	8.5264
4	7.7086	6.9443	6.5914	6.3882	6.2561	6.1631	6.0942	6.0410	5.9988	5.9644	5.9117	5.8578	5.8025	5.7744	5.7459	5.7170	5.6877	5.6581	5.6281
5	6.6079	5.7861	5.4095	5.1922	5.0503	4.9503	4.8759	4.8183	4.7725	4.7351	4.6777	4.6188	4.5581	4.5272	4.4957	4.4638	4.4314	4.3985	4.3650
6	5.9874	5.1433	4.7571	4.5337	4.3874	4.2839	4.2067	4.1468	4.0990	4.0600	3.9999	3.9381	3.8742	3.8415	3.8082	3.7743	3.7398	3.7047	3.6689
7	5.5914	4.7374	4.3468	4.1203	3.9715	3.8660	3.7870	3.7257	3.6767	3.6365	3.5747	3.5107	3.4445	3.4105	3.3758	3.3404	3.3043	3.2674	3.2298
8	5.3177	4.4590	4.0662	3.8379	3.6875	3.5806	3.5005	3.4381	3.3881	3.3472	3.2839	3.2184	3.1503	3.1152	3.0794	3.0428	3.0053	2.9669	2.9276
9	5.1174	4.2565	3.8625	3.6331	3.4817	3.3738	3.2927	3.2296	3.1789	3.1373	3.0729	3.0061	2.9365	2.9005	2.8637	2.8259	2.7872	2.7475	2.7067
10	4.9646	4.1028	3.7083	3.4780	3.3258	3.2172	3.1355	3.0717	3.0204	2.9782	2.9130	2.8450	2.7740	2.7372	2.6996	2.6609	2.6211	2.5801	2.5379
11	4.8443	3.9823	3.5874	3.3567	3.2039	3.0946	3.0123	2.9480	2.8962	2.8536	2.7876	2.7186	2.6464	2.6090	2.5705	2.5309	2.4901	2.4480	2.4045
12	4.7472	3.8853	3.4903	3.2592	3.1059	2.9961	2.9134	2.8486	2.7964	2.7534	2.6866	2.6169	2.5436	2.5055	2.4663	2.4259	2.3842	2.3410	2.2962
13	4.6672	3.8056	3.4105	3.1791	3.0254	2.9153	2.8321	2.7669	2.7144	2.6710	2.6037	2.5331	2.4589	2.4202	2.3803	2.3392	2.2966	2.2524	2.2064
14	4.6001	3.7389	3.3439	3.1122	2.9582	2.8477	2.7642	2.6987	2.6458	2.6022	2.5342	2.4630	2.3879	2.3487	2.3082	2.2664	2.2229	2.1778	2.1307
15	4.5431	3.6823	3.2874	3.0556	2.9013	2.7905	2.7066	2.6408	2.5876	2.5437	2.4753	2.4034	2.3275	2.2878	2.2468	2.2043	2.1601	2.1141	2.0658
16	4.4940	3.6337	3.2389	3.0069	2.8524	2.7413	2.6572	2.5911	2.5377	2.4935	2.4247	2.3522	2.2756	2.2354	2.1938	2.1507	2.1058	2.0589	2.0096
17	4.4513	3.5915	3.1968	2.9647	2.8100	2.6987	2.6143	2.5480	2.4943	2.4499	2.3807	2.3077	2.2304	2.1898	2.1477	2.1040	2.0584	2.0107	1.9604
18	4.4139	3.5546	3.1599	2.9277	2.7729	2.6613	2.5767	2.5102	2.4563	2.4117	2.3421	2.2686	2.1906	2.1497	2.1071	2.0629	2.0166	1.9681	1.9168
19	4.3807	3.5219	3.1274	2.8951	2.7401	2.6283	2.5435	2.4768	2.4227	2.3779	2.3080	2.2341	2.1555	2.1141	2.0712	2.0264	1.9795	1.9302	1.8780
20	4.3512	3.4928	3.0984	2.8661	2.7109	2.5990	2.5140	2.4471	2.3928	2.3479	2.2776	2.2033	2.1242	2.0825	2.0391	1.9938	1.9464	1.8963	1.8432
21	4.3248	3.4668	3.0725	2.8401	2.6848	2.5727	2.4876	2.4205	2.3660	2.3210	2.2504	2.1757	2.0960	2.0540	2.0102	1.9645	1.9165	1.8657	1.8117
22	4.3009	3.4434	3.0491	2.8167	2.6613	2.5491	2.4638	2.3965	2.3419	2.2967	2.2258	2.1508	2.0707	2.0283	1.9842	1.9380	1.8894	1.8380	1.7831
23	4.2793	3.4221	3.0280	2.7955	2.6400	2.5277	2.4422	2.3748	2.3201	2.2747	2.2036	2.1282	2.0476	2.0050	1.9605	1.9139	1.8648	1.8128	1.7570
24	4.2597	3.4028	3.0088	2.7763	2.6207	2.5082	2.4226	2.3551	2.3002	2.2547	2.1834	2.1077	2.0267	1.9838	1.9390	1.8920	1.8424	1.7896	1.7330
25	4.2417	3.3852	2.9912	2.7587	2.6030	2.4904	2.4047	2.3371	2.2821	2.2365	2.1649	2.0889	2.0075	1.9643	1.9192	1.8718	1.8217	1.7684	1.7110
26	4.2252	3.3690	2.9752	2.7426	2.5868	2.4741	2.3883	2.3205	2.2655	2.2197	2.1479	2.0716	1.9898	1.9464	1.9010	1.8533	1.8027	1.7488	1.6906
27	4.2100	3.3541	2.9604	2.7278	2.5719	2.4591	2.3732	2.3053	2.2501	2.2043	2.1323	2.0558	1.9736	1.9299	1.8842	1.8361	1.7851	1.7306	1.6717
28	4.1960	3.3404	2.9467	2.7141	2.5581	2.4453	2.3593	2.2913	2.2360	2.1900	2.1179	2.0411	1.9586	1.9147	1.8687	1.8203	1.7689	1.7138	1.6541
29	4.1830	3.3277	2.9340	2.7014	2.5454	2.4324	2.3463	2.2783	2.2229	2.1768	2.1045	2.0275	1.9446	1.9005	1.8543	1.8055	1.7537	1.6981	1.6376
30	4.1709	3.3158	2.9223	2.6896	2.5336	2.4205	2.3343	2.2662	2.2107	2.1646	2.0921	2.0148	1.9317	1.8874	1.8409	1.7918	1.7396	1.6835	1.6223
40	4.0847	3.2317	2.8387	2.6060	2.4495	2.3359	2.2490	2.1802	2.1240	2.0772	2.0035	1.9245	1.8389	1.7929	1.7444	1.6928	1.6373	1.5766	1.5089
60	4.0012	3.1504	2.7581	2.5252	2.3683	2.2541	2.1665	2.0970	2.0401	1.9926	1.9174	1.8364	1.7480	1.7001	1.6491	1.5943	1.5343	1.4673	1.3893
120	3.9201	3.0718	2.6802	2.4472	2.2899	2.1750	2.0868	2.0164	1.9588	1.9105	1.8337	1.7505	1.6587	1.6084	1.5543	1.4952	1.4290	1.3519	1.2539
∞	3.8415	2.9957	2.6049	2.3719	2.2141	2.0986	2.0096	1.9384	1.8799	1.8307	1.7522	1.6664	1.5705	1.5173	1.4591	1.3940	1.3180	1.2214	1.0000

Final Words

It is very difficult to formulate the words of the final conclusion.
ALWAYS consult this flowchart to determine the correct wording.

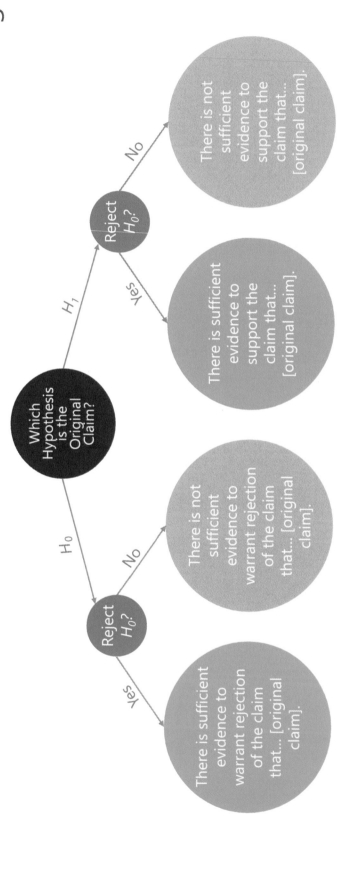

Glossary for the Triola Statistics Series

Acceptance sampling Sampling items and rejecting the whole batch based on the number of defects obtained.

Actual odds against The ratio $P(\overline{A})/P(A)$, usually expressed in the form of $a{:}b$ (or "a to b").

Actual odds in favor The reciprocal of the actual odds against an event.

Addition rule Rule for determining the probability that, on a single trial, either event A occurs, or event B occurs, or they both occur.

Adjusted coefficient of determination Multiple coefficient of determination R^2 modified to account for the number of variables and sample size.

Alpha (α) Symbol used to represent the probability of a type I error. *See also* Significance level.

Alternative hypothesis Statement that is equivalent to the negation of the null hypothesis; denoted by H_1

Analysis of variance Method of analyzing population variances in order to test hypotheses about equality of means of populations.

ANOVA *See* Analysis of variance.

Arithmetic mean Sum of a set of values divided by the number of values; usually referred to as the mean.

Assignable variation Type of variation in a process that results from causes that can be identified.

Attribute data Data that can be separated into different categories distinguished by some nonnumeric characteristic.

Average Any one of several measures designed to reveal the center of a collection of data.

Bar graph Uses bars of equal width to show frequencies of categories of data.

Bayes; Theorem Used for revising a probability value based on additional information that is later received.

Beta (β) Symbol used to represent the probability of a type II error.

Bimodal Having two modes.

Binomial experiment Experiment with a fixed number of independent trials, where each outcome falls into exactly one of two categories.

Binomial probability formula Expression used to calculate probabilities in a binomial experiment (see Formula 5-5 in Section 5-2).

Bivariate data Data arranged as matched pairs.

Bivariate normal distribution Distribution of paired data in which, for any fixed value of one variable, the values of the other variable are normally distributed.

Blinding Procedure used in experiments whereby the subject doesn't know whether he or she is receiving a treatment or a placebo.

Block A group of subjects that are similar in the ways that might affect the outcome of an experiment.

Bootstrap Sample A random sample obtained by selecting values from the original sample with replacement.

Box-and-whisker diagram *See* Boxplot.

Boxplot Graphical representation of the spread of a set of data

Case-control study Study in which data are collected from the past by going back in time (through examination of records, interviews, and so on).

Categorical data Data that can be separated into different categories that are distinguished by some nonnumeric characteristic.

Cell Category used to separate qualitative (or attribute) data.

Census Collection of data from every element in a population.

Centerline Line used in a control chart to represent a central value of the characteristic measurements.

Central limit theorem Theorem stating that sample means tend to be normally distributed with mean μ and standard deviation $\sigma/\sqrt{n}$.

Centroid The point $(\bar{x}, \bar{y})$ determined from a collection of bivariate data.

Chebyshev's theorem Theorem that uses the standard deviation to provide information about the distribution of data.

Chi-square distribution A continuous probability distribution used for inferences about a standard deviation or variance and for goodness-of-fit and contingency tables.

Class boundaries Values obtained from a frequency distribution by increasing the upper class limits and decreasing the lower class limits by the same amount so that there are no gaps between consecutive classes.

Classical approach to probability Approach in which the probability of an event is determined by dividing the number of ways the event can occur by the total number of possible outcomes.

Class midpoint In a class of a frequency distribution, the value midway between the lower class limit and the upper class limit.

Class width The difference between two consecutive lower class limits in a frequency distribution.

Cluster sampling Dividing the population area into sections (or clusters), then randomly selecting a few of those sections, and then choosing *all* the members from those selected sections.

Coefficient of determination Amount of the variation in *y* that is explained by the regression line.

Coefficient of variation (or CV) The ratio of the standard deviation to the mean, expressed as a percent.

Cohort study Study of subjects in identified groups sharing common factors (called *cohorts*), with data collected in the future.

Combinations rule Rule for determining the number of different combinations of selected items.

Complement of an event All outcomes in which the original event does not occur.

Completely randomized design Procedure in an experiment whereby each element is given the same chance of belonging to the different categories or treatments.

Compound event Combination of simple events.

Conditional probability The probability of an event, given that some other event has already occurred.

Confidence coefficient Probability that a population parameter is contained within a particular confidence interval; also called confidence level or degree of confidence.

Confidence interval Range of values used to estimate some population parameter with a specific confidence level; also called an interval estimate.

Confidence interval limits Two numbers that are used as the high and low boundaries of a confidence interval.

Confidence level Probability that a particular confidence interval actually contains a population parameter.

Confounding A situation that occurs when the effects from two or more variables cannot be distinguished from each other.

Contingency table Table of observed frequencies where the rows correspond to one variable of classification and the columns correspond to another variable of classification; also called a two-way table.

Continuity correction Adjustment made when a discrete random variable is being approximated by a continuous random variable.

Continuous data Data resulting from infinitely many possible values that correspond to some continuous scale that covers a range of values without gaps, interruptions, or jumps.

Continuous random variable A random variable with infinitely many values that can be associated with points on a continuous line interval.

Control chart Any one of several types of charts depicting some characteristic of a process in order to determine whether there is statistical stability.

Control group A group of subjects in an experiment who are not given a particular treatment.

Control limit Boundary used in a control chart for identifying unusual points.

Convenience sampling Sampling in which data are selected because they are readily available.

Correlation Statistical association between two variables.

Correlation coefficient Measurement of the strength of the relationship between two variables.

Critical region The set of all values of the test statistic that would cause rejection of the null hypothesis.

Critical value Value separating the critical region from the values of the test statistic that would not lead to rejection of the null hypothesis.

Critical value method of testing hypotheses Method of testing hypotheses based on a comparison of the test statistic and critical values.

Cross-sectional study Study in which data are observed, measured, and collected at one point in time.

Cumulative frequency Sum of the frequencies for a class and all preceding classes.

Cumulative frequency distribution Frequency distribution in which each class and frequency represents cumulative data up to and including that class.

Data Numbers or information describing some characteristic.

Degree of confidence Probability that a particular confidence interval actually contains a population parameter; also called level of confidence.

Degrees of freedom Number of values that are free to vary after certain restrictions have been imposed on all values.

Denominator degrees of freedom Degrees of freedom corresponding to the denominator of the F test statistic.

Density curve Graph of a continuous probability distribution.

Dependent events Events for which the occurrence of any one event affects the probabilities of the occurrences of the other events.

Dependent sample Sample whose values are related to the values in another sample.

Dependent variable y variable in a regression or multiple regression equation.

Descriptive statistics Methods used to summarize the key characteristics of known data.

Deviation Amount of difference between a value and the mean; expressed as $x - \bar{x}$.

Dichotomous variable Variable which has two possible discrete values.

Discordant pairs Pairs of categories in which the two categories are different; used in McNemar's test.

Discrete data Data with the property that the number of possible values is either a finite number or a "countable" number, which results in 0 possibilities, or 1 possibility, or 2 possibilities, and so on.

Discrete random variable Random variable with either a finite number of values or a countable number of values.

Disjoint events Events that cannot occur simultaneously

Distribution-free tests Tests not requiring a particular distribution, such as the normal distribution. *See also* Nonparametric tests.

Dotplot Graph in which each data value is plotted as a point (or dot) along a scale of values.

Double-blind Procedure used in an experiment whereby the subject doesn't know whether he or she is receiving a treatment or placebo, and the person administering the treatment also does not know.

Dummy variable A dichotomous variable with the two possible values of 0 and 1. Used in multiple regression.

Efficiency Measure of the sensitivity of a nonparametric test in comparison to a corresponding parametric test.

Empirical rule Rule that uses standard deviation to provide information about data with a bell-shaped distribution.

Estimate Specific value or range of values used to approximate some population parameter.

Estimator Sample statistic (such as the sample mean $\bar{x}$, used to approximate a population parameter.

Event Result or outcome of an experiment.

Expected frequency Theoretical frequency for a cell of a contingency table or multinomial table.

Expected value For a discrete random variable, the mean value of the outcomes.

Experiment Application of some treatment followed by observation of its effects on the subjects.

Experimental units Subjects in an experiment.

Explained deviation For one pair of values in a collection of bivariate data, the difference between the predicted y value and the mean of the y values.

Explained variation Sum of the squares of the explained deviations for all pairs of bivariate data in a sample.

Exploratory data analysis (EDA) Branch of statistics emphasizing the investigation of data.

Factor In analysis of variance, a property or characteristic that allows us to distinguish the different populations from one another.

Factorial rule Rule stating that n different items can be arranged $n!$ different ways.

F distribution Continuous probability distribution used for inferences involving two standard deviations or variances..

Finite population correction factor Factor for correcting the standard error of the mean when a sample size exceeds 5% of the size of a finite population.

Five-number summary Minimum value, maximum value, median, and the first and third quartiles of a set of data.

Fractiles Numbers that partition data into parts that are approximately equal in size.

Frequency distribution Listing of data values (either individually or by groups of intervals), along with their corresponding frequencies (or counts).

Frequency polygon Graphical representation of the distribution of data using connected straight-line segments.

Frequency distribution List of categories of values along with their corresponding frequencies.

Frequency table *See* frequency distribution.

Fundamental counting rule Rule stating that, for a sequence of two events in which the first event can occur m ways and the second can occur n ways, the events together can occur a total of $m \cdot n$ ways.

Goodness-of-fit test Test for how well some observed frequency distribution fits some claimed distribution.

Histogram Graph of vertical bars representing the frequency distribution of a set of data.

H test The nonparametric Kruskal-Wallis test.

Hypothesis Statement or claim about some property of a population.

Hypothesis test Method for testing claims made about populations; also called test of significance.

Independent events Events for which the occurrence of any one of the events does not affect the probabilities of the occurrences of the other events.

Independent sample Sample whose values are not related to the values in another sample.

Independent variable The x variable in a regression equation, or one of the x variables in a multiple regression equation.

Inferential statistics Methods involving the use of sample data to make generalizations or inferences about a population.

Influential point Point that strongly affects the graph of a regression line.

Interaction In two-way analysis of variance, the effect when one of the factors changes for different categories of the other factor.

Interquartile range The difference between the first and third quartiles.

Interval Level of measurement of data; characterizes data that can be arranged in order and for which differences between data values are meaningful.

Interval estimate Range of values used to estimate some population parameter with a specific level of confidence; also called a confidence interval.

Kruskal-Wallis test Nonparametric hypothesis test used to compare three or more independent samples; also called an H test.

Law of large numbers As a procedure is repeated, the relative frequency probability of an event tends to approach the actual proability.

Least-squares property Property stating that, for a regression line, the sum of the squares of the vertical deviations of the sample points from the regression line is the smallest sum possible.

Left-tailed test Hypothesis test in which the critical region is located in the extreme left area of the probability distribution.

Level of confidence Probability that a particular confidence interval actually contains a population parameter; also called degree of confidence.

Linear correlation coefficient Measure of the strength of the relationship between two variables.

Logistic regression Method used in multiple regression when the dummy variable is the response (y) variable.

Longitudinal study Study of subjects in identified groups sharing common factors (called *cohorts*), with data collected in the future.

Lower class limits Smallest numbers that can actually belong to the different classes in a frequency distribution.

Lower control limit Boundary used in a control chart to separate points that are unusually low.

Lurking variable Variable that affects the variables being studied, but is not itself included in the study.

Mann-Whitney *U* test Hypothesis test equivalent to the Wilcoxon rank-sum test for two independent samples.

Marginal change For variables related by a regression equation, the amount of change in the dependent variable when one of the independent variables changes by one unit and the other independent variables remain constant.

Margin of error Maximum likely (with probability $1 - \alpha$) difference between the observed sample statistic and the true value of the population parameter.

Matched pairs With two samples, there is some relationship so that each value in one sample is paired with a corresponding value in the other sample.

Mathematical model Mathematical function that "fits" or describes real-world data.

Maximum error of estimate *See* Margin of error.

McNemar's test Uses frequency counts from matched pairs of nominal data from two categories to test the null hypothesis that the frequencies from discordant pairs occur in the same proportion.

Mean The sum of a set of values divided by the number of values.

Mean absolute deviation Measure of variation equal to the sum of absolute value of the deviation of each value from the mean, divided by the number of values.

Measure of center Value intended to indicate the center of the values in a collection of data.

Measure of variation Any of several measures designed to reflect the amount of variation or spread for a set of values.

Median Middle value of a set of values arranged in order of magnitude.

Midquartile One-half of the sum of the first and third quartiles.

Midrange One-half the sum of the highest and lowest values.

Mode Value that occurs most frequently.

Modified boxplot Boxplot constructed with these modifications: (1) A special symbol (such as an asterisk or point) is used to identify outliers, and (2) the solid horizontal line extends only as far as the minimum data value that is not an outlier and the maximum data value that is not an outlier.

MS(error) Mean square for error; used in analysis of variance.

MS(total) Mean square for total variation; used in analysis of variance.

MS(treatment) Mean square for treatments; used in analysis of variance.

Multimodal Having more than two modes.

Multinomial experiment Experiment with a fixed number of independent trials, where each outcome falls into exactly one of several categories.

Multiple coefficient of determination Measure of how well a multiple regression equation fits the sample data.

Multiple comparison procedures Procedures for identifying which particular means are different, after concluding that three or more means are not all equal.

Multiple regression Study of linear relationships among three or more variables.

Multiple regression equation Equation that expresses a linear relationship between a dependent variable y and two or more independent variables $(x_1, x_2, \ldots, x_k)$.

Multiplication rule Rule for determining the probability that event A will occur on one trial and event B will occur on a second trial.

Mutually exclusive events Events that cannot occur simultaneously.

Negatively skewed Skewed to the left.

Nominal Level of measurement of data; characterizes data that consist of names, labels, or categories only.

Nonparametric tests Statistical procedures for testing hypotheses or estimating parameters, where there are no required assumptions about the nature or shape of population distributions; also called distribution-free tests.

Nonsampling errors Errors from external factors not related to sampling.

Normal distribution Bell-shaped probability distribution described algebraically by Formula 6-1 in Section 6-1.

Normal quantile plot Graph of points (x, y), where each x value is from the original set of sample data, and each y value is a z score corresponding to a quantile value of the standard normal distribution.

np chart Control chart in which numbers of defects are plotted so that a process can be monitored.

Null hypothesis Claim made about some population characteristic, usually involving the case of no difference; denoted by H_0.

Numerator degrees of freedom Degrees of freedom corresponding to the numerator of the F test statistic.

Numerical data Data consisting of numbers representing counts or measurements.

Observational study Study in which we observe and measure specific characteristics, but don't attempt to manipulate or modify the subjects being studied.

Observed frequency Actual frequency count recorded in one cell of a contingency table or multinomial table.

Odds against Ratio of the probability of an event not occurring to the event occurring, usually expressed in the form of $a:b$ where a and b are integers having no common factors.

Odds in favor Ratio of the probability of an event occurring to the event not occurring, usually expressed as the ratio of two integers with no common factors.

One-way analysis of variance Analysis of variance involving data classified into groups according to a single criterion only.

Ordinal Level of measurement of data; characterizes data that may be arranged in order, but differences between data values either cannot be determined or are meaningless.

Outliers Values that are very unusual in the sense that they are very far away from most of the data.

Paired samples Two samples that are dependent in the sense that the data values are matched by pairs.

Parameter Measured characteristic of a population.

Parametric tests Statistical procedures, based on population parameters, for testing hypotheses or estimating parameters.

Pareto chart Bar graph for qualitative data, with the bars arranged in order according to frequencies.

Payoff odds Ratio of net profit (if you win) to the amount bet.

p chart Control chart used to monitor the proportion p for some attribute in a process.

Pearson's product moment correlation coefficient *See* Linear correlation coefficient.

Percentile The 99 values that divide ranked data into 100 groups with approximately 1% of the values in each group.

Permutations rule Rule for determining the number of different arrangements of selected items.

Pie chart Graphical representation of data in the form of a circle containing wedges.

Placebo effect Effect that occurs when an untreated subject incorrectly believes that he or she is receiving a real treatment and reports an improvement in symptoms.

Point estimate Single value that serves as an estimate of a population parameter.

Poisson distribution Discrete probability distribution that applies to occurrences of some event over a specified interval of time, distance, area, volume, or some similar unit.

Pooled estimate of p_1 and p_2 Probability obtained by combining the data from two sample proportions and dividing the total number of successes by the total number of observations.

Pooled estimate of σ^2 Estimate of the variance σ^2 that is common to two populations, found by computing a weighted average of the two sample variances.

Population Complete and entire collection of elements to be studied.

Positively skewed Skewed to the right.

Power of a test Probability $(1 - \beta)$ of rejecting a false null hypothesis.

Predicted values Values of a dependent variable found by using values of independent variables in a regression equation.

Prediction interval Confidence interval estimate of a predicted value of *y*.

Predictor variables Independent variables in a regression equation.

Probability Measure of the likelihood that a given event will occur; expressed as a number between 0 and 1.

Probability distribution Collection of values of a random variable along with their corresponding probabilities.

Probability histogram Histogram with outcomes listed along the horizontal axis and probabilities listed along the vertical axis.

Probability sample Sample selected so that each member of the population has a know (but not necessarily the same) chance of being selected.

Probability value *See* P-value.

Process data Data, arranged according to some time sequence, that measure a characteristic of goods or services resulting from some combination of equipment, people, materials, methods, and conditions.

Prospective study Study of subjects in identified groups sharing common factors (called *cohorts*), with data collected in the future.

***P*-value** Probability that a test statistic in a hypothesis test is at least as extreme as the one actually obtained.

***P*-value method of hypothesis testing** Method of hypothesis testing based on a comparison of the *P*-value and the level of significance.

Qualitative data Data that can be separated into different categories distinguished by some nonnumeric characteristic.

Quantitative data Data consisting of numbers representing counts or measurements.

Quartiles The three values that divide ranked data into four groups with approximately 25% of the values in each group.

Randomized block design Design in which a measurement is obtained for each treatment on each of several individuals matched according to similar characteristics.

Random sample Sample selected in a way that allows every member of the population to have the same chance of being chosen.

Random selection Selection of sample elements in such a way that all elements available for selection have the same chance of being selected.

Random variable Variable (typically represented by *x*) that has a single numerical value (determined by chance) for each outcome of an experiment.

Random variation Type of variation in a process that is due to chance; the type of variation inherent in any process not capable of producing every good or service exactly the same way every time.

Range The measure of variation that is the difference between the highest and lowest values.

Range chart Control chart based on sample ranges; used to monitor variation in a process.

Range rule of thumb Rule based on the principle that for typical data sets, the difference between the lowest typical value and the highest typical value is approximately 4 standard deviations ($4s$).

Rank Numerical position of an item in a sample set arranged in order.

Rank correlation coefficient Measure of the strength of the relationship between two variables; based on the ranks of the values.

Rare event rule If, under a given assumption, the probability of a particular observed result is extremely small, we conclude that the assumption is probably not correct.

Ratio Level of measurement of data; characterizes data that can be arranged in order, for which differences between data values are meaningful, and there is an inherent zero starting point.

R chart Control chart based on sample ranges; used to monitor variation in a process.

Regression equation Algebraic equation describing the relationship among variables.

Regression line Straight line that best fits a collection of points representing paired sample data.

Relative frequency Frequency for a class, divided by the total of all frequencies.

Relative frequency approximation of probability Estimated value of probability based on actual observations.

Relative frequency distribution Variation of the basic frequency distribution in which the frequency for each class is divided by the total of all frequencies.

Relative frequency histogram Variation of the basic histogram in which frequencies are replaced by relative frequencies.

Replication Repetition of an experiment.

Residual Difference between an observed sample y value and the value of y that is predicted from a regression equation.

Response variable y variable in a regression or multiple regression equation.

Retrospective study Study in which data are collected from the past by going back in time (through examination of records, interviews, and so on).

Right-tailed test Hypothesis test in which the critical region is located in the extreme right area of the probability distribution.

Rigorously controlled design Design of experiment in which all factors are forced to be constant so that effects of extraneous factors are eliminated.

Run Sequence of data exhibiting the same characteristic; used in runs test for randomness.

Run chart Sequential plot of individual data values over time, where one axis (usually the vertical axis) is used for the data values and the other axis (usually the horizontal axis) is used for the time sequence.

Runs test Nonparametric method used to test for randomness.

Sample Subset of a population.

Sample size Number of items in a sample.

Sample space Set of all possible outcomes or events in an experiment that cannot be further broken down.

Sampling distribution of proportion The probability distribution of sample proportions, with all samples having the same sample size n.

Sampling distribution of sample means Distribution of the sample means that is obtained when we repeatedly draw samples of the same size from the same population.

Sampling error Difference between a sample result and the true population result; results from chance sample fluctuations.

Sampling variability Variation of a statistic in different samples.

Scatter diagram Graphical display of paired (x, y) data.

Scatterplot Graphical display of paired (x, y) data.

***s* chart** Control chart, based on sample standard deviations, that is used to monitor variation in a process

Self-selected sample Sample in which the respondents themselves decide whether to be included; also called voluntary response sample.

Semi-interquartile range One-half of the difference between the first and third quartiles.

Significance level Probability of making a type I error when conducting a hypothesis test.

Sign test Nonparametric hypothesis test used to compare samples from two populations.

Simple event Experimental outcome that cannot be further broken down.

Simple random sample Sample of a particular size selected so that every possible sample of the same size has the same chance of being chosen.

Simulation Process that behaves in a way that is similar to some experiment so that similar results are produced.

Single factor analysis of variance *See* One-way analysis of variance.

Skewed Not symmetric and extending more to one side than the other.

Slope Measure of steepness of a straight line.

Sorted data Data arranged in order.

Spearman's rank correlation coefficient *See* Rank correlation coefficient.

SS(error) Sum of squares representing the variability that is assumed to be common to all the populations being considered; used in analysis of variance.

SS(total) Measure of the total variation (around $\bar{\bar{x}}$) in all of the sample data combined; used in analysis of variance.

SS(treatment) Measure of the variation between the sample means; used in analysis of variance.

Standard deviation Measure of variation equal to the square root of the variance.

Standard error of estimate Measure of spread of sample points about the regression line.

Standard error of the mean Standard deviation of all possible sample means $\bar{x}$.

Standard normal distribution Normal distribution with a mean of 0 and a standard deviation equal to 1.

Standard score Number of standard deviations that a given value is above or below the mean; also called *z* score.

Statistic Measured characteristic of a sample.

Statistically stable process Process with only natural variation and no patterns, cycles, or unusual points.

Statistical process control (SPC) Use of statistical techniques such as control charts to analyze a process or its outputs so as to take appropriate actions to achieve and maintain a state of statistical control and to improve the process capability.

Statistics Collection of methods for planning experiments, obtaining data, organizing, summarizing, presenting, analyzing, interpreting, and drawing conclusions based on data.

Stem-and-Leaf plot *See* stemplot.

Stemplot Method of sorting and arranging data to reveal the distribution.

Stepwise regression Process of using different combinations of variables until the best model is obtained; used in multiple regression.

Stratified sampling Sampling in which samples are drawn from each stratum (class).

Student *t* distribution *See t* distribution.

Subjective probability Guess or estimate of a probability based on knowledge of relevant circumstances.

Symmetric Property of data for which the distribution can be divided into two halves that are approximately mirror images by drawing a vertical line through the middle.

Systematic sampling Sampling in which every kth element is selected.

t distribution Bell-shaped distribution usually associated with sample data from a population with an unknown standard deviation.

10–90 percentile range Difference between the 10th and 90th percentiles.

Test of homogeneity Test of the claim that different populations have the same proportion of some characteristic.

Test of independence Test of the null hypothesis that for a contingency table, the row variable and column variable are not related.

Test of significance *See* Hypothesis test.

Test statistic Sample statistic based on the sample data; used in making the decision about rejection of the null hypothesis.

Time-series data Data that have been collected at different points in time.

Total deviation Sum of the explained deviation and unexplained deviation for a given pair of values in a collection of bivariate data.

Total variation Sum of the squares of the total deviation for all pairs of bivariate data in a sample.

Treatment Property or characteristic that allows us to distinguish the different populations from one another; used in analysis of variance.

Treatment group Group of subjects given some treatment in an experiment.

Tree diagram Graphical depiction of the different possible outcomes in a compound event.

Two-tailed test Hypothesis test in which the critical region is divided between the left and right extreme areas of the probability distribution.

Two-way analysis of variance Analysis of variance involving data classified according to two different factors.

Two-way table *See* Contingency table.

Type I error Mistake of rejecting the null hypothesis when it is true.

Type II error Mistake of failing to reject the null hypothesis when it is false.

Unbiased estimator Sample statistic that tends to target the population parameter that it is used to estimate.

Unexplained deviation For one pair of values in a collection of bivariate data, the difference between the y coordinate and the predicted value.

Unexplained variation Sum of the squares of the unexplained deviations for all pairs of bivariate data in a sample.

Uniform distribution Probability distribution in which every value of the random variable is equally likely.

Upper class limits Largest numbers that can belong to the different classes in a frequency distribution.

Upper control limit Boundary used in a control chart to separate points that are unusually high.

Variance Measure of variation equal to the square of the standard deviation.

Variance between samples In analysis of variance, the variation among the different samples.

Variation due to error *See* Variation within samples.

Variation due to treatment *See* Variance between samples.

Variation within samples In analysis of variance, the variation that is due to chance.

Voluntary response sample Sample in which the respondents themselves decide whether to be included.

Weighted mean Mean of a collection of values that have been assigned different degrees of importance.

Wilcoxon rank-sum test Nonparametric hypothesis test used to compare two independent samples.

Wilcoxon signed-ranks test Nonparametric hypothesis test used to compare two dependent samples.

Within statistical control *See* Statistically stable process.

$\bar{x}$ **chart** Control chart used to monitor the mean of a process.

y-intercept Point at which a straight line crosses the *y*-axis.

z score Number of standard deviations that a given value is above or below the mean.